Christ
Our High Priest

LET US
CONFIDENTLY WELCOME

Christ
Our High Priest

Spiritual Exercises with Pope Benedict XVI

CARDINAL ALBERT VANHOYE

GRACEWING

Originally published in Australia by Modotti Press
(Connor Court Publishing)

First published in the European Union in 2010

Gracewing
2 Southern Avenue, Leominster
Herefordshire HR6 0QF
United Kingdom

ISBN 978 085244 768 0

Front cover: Ian James

Typesetting by Connor Court Publishing

This book is dedicated to all Christians who seek the priestly face of Christ.

Contents

Spiritual Exercises with Pope Benedict XVI
Preached in the Vatican February 10–16, 2008

Introduction[1]

The God of the Bible is not a mute God: he is a God who speaks to men so as to enter into communication and even into communion with them. In earlier times, in the Old Covenant, he accomplished this plan through the prophets and the levitical priesthood. In the "fullness of time", however, he sent his own Son, who was not just a bearer of the Word as were the prophets; he is the Word of God himself, the *Logos* incarnate (*Jn* 1:1). This Son, by his death and resurrection, has established a new priesthood, the perfect mediation between God and man, true communion. The theme of these Exercises is the acceptance of Christ's priestly mediation in our faith and in our life.

---

1 Due to the nature of the text, which abounds not only in proper nouns of people and places of biblical history but also in terms often capitalised in a devotional context, this English translation uses minimal capitalisation in the case of the latter category, following the author's own style. The scriptural references in brackets are provided in a regular, abbreviated form due to their proliferation. At times the author, who is an accomplished teacher, expresses the same idea in two or three different ways. It will be helpful to the reader to keep in mind that these chapters were prepared for preaching Spiritual Exercises. Due to the nature of their content, as well as the background expertise of their author, these "exercises" might well be called: "Spiritual Exercises of Christ the Priest".

HS
↓
Ras priest

1
"God has spoken to us"
(Hb 1:1-2)[2]

Eminences, Most Reverent Bishops, Monsignors:

With a sense of humility and united to the gentle heart of our Lord, I rejoice to be at your service for these Spiritual Exercises. There are many topics that I would like to put before you but I am reassured by the awareness that I am not the main actor. In Spiritual Exercises, the principal actor is clearly the Holy Spirit; otherwise they would not merit to be called *Spiritual* Exercises. Therefore, I suggest to you that, above all, we entrust ourselves with great openness to the guidance of the Holy Spirit who will bring us to understand the Word of God deeply. He will unite us interiorly with the Heart of Christ, pouring into our hearts the love which comes from God, as the Apostle, St Paul, says (*Rm* 5:5). The Holy Spirit will also accomplish his work of purification, which we are always in need of, as well as his mission of illumination, by showing us more precisely our way of love and service for this Lent and the months that will follow.

The theme of these Exercises will be the acceptance of Christ's priestly mediation in our faith and in our life. Let us confidently welcome Christ our High Priest! In confronting this topic, I will be inspired above all, naturally, by the Letter to the Hebrews, which presents Christ to us as our High Priest and introduces us to a profound understanding of his priestly oblation and mediation. The author of the Letter to the Hebrews, who

---

2 All Scripture quotations are taken from the Revised Standard Version, Catholic Edition.

seems to be a companion of Paul's, a travelling apostle, has made a passing exposé of Psalm 109/110, from the first oracle in the first verse to the second oracle in the fourth verse. This psalm which we recite, chant or sing – it is sung every Sunday at Vespers – contains the oracle: "The Lord said to my Lord: sit at my right hand." It is an oracle that Jesus applied to himself during his interrogation before the Sanhedrin (*Mt* 26:64ff) and which St Peter, in his first Pentecostal discourse, applied to the risen Jesus (*Acts* 2:34-35). It was, therefore, a tradition to apply this first oracle to Christ. It seems, however, that, before the author of the Letter to the Hebrews, no one had the idea of passing from the first verse to the fourth where there is a second oracle more solemn than the first because it is supported by a divine oath, "The Lord has sworn and he will not retract: you are a priest". The author has noted this and has deepened the theme intensely; in the light of it, he has contemplated again the mystery of Christ and discovered that in the theme of Christ's priesthood is truly contained the perfect fulfillment of precepts and of sacrifice.

In this first meditation, let us begin with the first verse of the Letter to the Hebrews, which is a magnificent text. The author does not speak about priesthood immediately but prepares for this topic with a very beautiful phrase:

> In many and various ways, God spoke of old to our fathers by the prophets, but in these days, he has spoken to us by a son whom he appointed heir of all things, through whom also he created the world (*Hb* 1:1).

As you can tell, this phrase is no way to begin a letter: it is the beginning of a homily. The so-called Letter to the Hebrews is not a letter, but a homily, a magnificent homily on the priesthood of Christ. It is a homily that was given in various communities because we shall see that the author was not himself the leader of a community (Cf. *Hb* 13:17) but a travelling apostle. Besides, the text was sent to a distant community with some accompanying rules and so, for this reason, the homily became known as the

Letter to the Hebrews.

The principle affirmation or statement is that God has spoken: God has spoken to the fathers in ancient times; God has spoken to us who are at the end of the ages. This statement is extraordinary in itself but we are so used to reading it, that it makes little impression. The God of the Bible is a God who speaks to men. He is not a mute God: he is a God who speaks to men in order to enter into communion with them. God has taken the initiative to establish a relationship with us, which has then become a priestly mediation in Christ. We must note that in this phrase the author does not express the content of the divine message. That is, he does not choose a series of truths that God would have communicated to us.

Revelation is often spoken of as a combination of truths to which one must adhere with faith. But here, for the author of the Letter to the Hebrews, it is not the most important aspect. The important thing for him is that God has put himself in communication with us. To speak with a person is always to establish a relationship. It is true that in some cases, the objective content of the message can have more importance than the relationship. For example, in commercial correspondence, the persons involved do not have the primary importance. Rather, the object or the affair that is treated matters most. Instead, when a letter is written to a friend, its content can be secondary: what matters firstly is the personal relationship. The purpose of such a letter is not so much to communicate news as to maintain and nourish an affective relationship.

This was God's purpose precisely. He spoke to us by entering into communion with us. That a God so great, so holy, so different from us has made the initiative to reveal himself to us by establishing a relationship with us and by deepening it is an extraordinary thing. God has spoken to us. God speaks to us: this is truly amazing. We must become aware of the extraordinary initiative of God. In these days, God wants to enter more

intensely and more intimately into a more profound and personal
relationship with each one of you. He wants to speak to your
heart as once he spoke to Israel his spouse: "I led you into the
desert and I spoke to your heart", says the prophet Hosea (2:16).
The characteristic of our God is that he is a God of covenant,
a God who wants to establish a personal relationship and to
continually deepen it. This is explained in the initial phrases of
the letter, not by indicating the content of the message but by
naming the persons involved: God who speaks; the receivers
of the divine message; the fathers of times long ago; we now;
the mediators of the word, the prophets in ancient times; the
Son now. We understand that sometimes people do not speak
because they want to avoid or delay entering into a relationship,
for various reasons: differences of social class, differences of
family or ethnic background, differences of opinion, etc. In this
sense, in John's Gospel, we see how a Samaritan woman is amazed
because Jesus speaks to her: "How is it that you, a Jew, ask me, a
Samaritan woman, for a drink?" (*Jn* 4:9). The evangelist explains
that between the Jews and the Samaritans, relationships are not
healthy: in effect, the Jews despised the Samaritans. The Book of
Sirach contains many harsh expressions against the Samaritans.
It says, "With two nations, my soul is vexed and the third is no
nation: those who live on Mount Seir and the Philistines and
the foolish people that live in Shekhom". However, Jesus breaks
through this barrier and he does so because he knows it is the will
of the Father. In order to explain his surprising behaviour to his
disciples, he will say, "My food is to do the will of Him who sent
me." (*Jn* 4:34). The will of God is to communicate with a view to
authentic communion. So as to bring this will to fulfillment in us,
he willed the priestly mediation of Christ.

There are some people who, although they once used to
speak, no longer speak to each other. Their relationships were
interrupted because offences were retained or they were treated
unjustly. God had so many reasons not to speak anymore to his

people who were unfaithful and obstinate, following their own ways instead of the ways of the Lord. However, we see in the Old Testament that God is never resigned to the breaking of relationships. He always wants to enter into communication with his people.

The author of the Letter to the Hebrews insists on the array of divine initiatives: "At many times and in many ways" are the first words of the Letter. We can indeed recall so many ways in which God has spoken to his people. The Old Testament is the history of God's Word. The covenant with Abraham begins with some words of the Lord. God spoke to Abraham, "Leave the house of your father and go to the country that I will point out to you. I will make of you a great people and I will bless you and I will make your name great and you will enjoy a great blessing" (*Gn* 12:1-2). These first words reveal various characteristics of the Word of God because they present two aspects: a great need and a marvellous generosity. The need is a need of love. It requires distance because distance is necessary in order to create a space that God can fill with his gifts. The Word of God for each one of us always has these two aspects: a great need of distance and a truly unconfined, unlimited generosity, "I will make of you a great nation, I will bless you, I will make your name great, you will enjoy a blessing". The Lord speaks to Moses in the burning bush and it is very interesting to see how God defines himself. He says to Moses, "I am the God of your fathers, the God of Abraham, the God of Isaac, and the God of Jacob" (*Ex* 3:6). God does not define himself in terms of his omnipotence. Neither does he define himself in terms of his omniscience. Rather, he defines himself by means of personal relationships with certain men of importance. Jeremiah frequently records that God never tires of sending his servants, the prophets, to his people to guide them, to admonish them, to exhort them and to give them promises (*Jr* 20:4, 29:19). God has used every possible means to establish discourse with his people.

The author of the Letter to the Hebrews distinguishes two periods of communication of the Word of God and two kinds of mediators. The first period is the ancient one: God has spoken in ancient times to the fathers by means of the prophets. The second is the eschatological period, the period of God's decisive intervention. The author literally says, "Now at the end of the ages, which are these". "At the end of the ages" is a biblical expression of the seventy weeks with which the decisive intervention of the Lord, at the end of time, was announced. The author was aware that this time has already come. We are in the eschatological time. God has intervened in a decisive way through his Son. It is not possible to imagine a more perfect mediator. Through his voice we hear the voice of the Father and are introduced into the Father's divine life. The Gospel of John tells us that the Son is not only a bearer of the Word of God as were the prophets, but that he *is* the Word *Ho Logos* (*Jn* 1:1), God incarnate. In him, we find the fullness of the Spirit. We are able to reflect on this marvellous event: Christ as mediator of the Word of God. The first step to establishing a covenant consists in being spoken to. It is not enough but it is fundamental. It is not enough because, for a covenant, blood is necessary; however, the Word manifests the meaning of the blood.

I invite you, therefore, to reflect on this divine generosity, manifested in his Word in the Gospel of today's Mass: Jesus shows us the importance of the Word of God, "Man does not live on bread alone but on every Word that comes from the mouth of God" (*Mt* 4:4; *Dt* 8:3). We are here to receive the Word of God and we have such need of help from the Holy Spirit to receive it well. We are also here to reconsider and to listen again to the history of the Word of God in our life, which is a very helpful way to be united with the Lord because in our life, the Word of God has been decisive in some moments: in our infancy, then in our adolescence and then again in our vocation. There are so many words from the Lord that have had a decisive influence on our life. Our recollection must end in a prayer of wonder: "What is man that thou art mindful of him, and the son of man that thou dost care for him?" (*Ps* 8:5) This quotation is within a particular prayer of love, and it is recognized as such. The Lord has communicated his Word to us; the Lord has placed himself in a profound relationship with us and we must deepen this relationship during these days. We must open our hearts to the Word of God with great confidence.

2
"God has spoken in his own Son"
(Hb 1:2-4)

We have meditated on the beginning of the Letter to the Hebrews. We saw how the author prepared the theme of the priestly mediation of Christ by speaking of the mediation of the Word, which is a fundamental aspect of priestly mediation. God "in many times and in various ways" (*Hb* 1:1) has put himself in communication with us; he has spoken to us: at first, through the prophets in the Old Testament; now in the eschatological period through his only begotten Son. No sooner is the person of the Son named, than the author seems fascinated by him. He contemplates him in his glory and can no longer speak of any other. The entire remainder of the very long opening sentence is dedicated to the description of the Son (*Hb* 1:2-4). By meditating on this sentence, we too want to be fascinated by the divine glory of the Son, with the joy of knowing that he has been given us by the Father as mediator of the Word, as priestly mediator, who puts us in an intimate communication with the Father. He is not concerned with the contemplation of a distant glory, but with the glory of him who introduces us to communion with God.

The first thing that the author says of the Son is the most unexpected in the sense that it could also be the last. He says that God "has constituted" the Son "the heir of all things" (*Hb* 1:2). An inheritance does not come at the beginning; it comes at the end. Nevertheless, the author contemplates the Son in the glory that he has now. This is always the case in the Letter to the Hebrews: at each new step, the author begins with the contemplation of Christ in the glory that he has now and this corresponds to the fundamental Christian experience which we must always renew in ourselves. After Easter and Pentecost, we are aware of being in an intimate relationship with the Heavenly Father through the glorified Christ. Christ, therefore, has been constituted the "heir of all things".

This affirmation corresponds to the risen Christ's declaration made at the end of St Matthew's Gospel. "All power has been given to me in heaven and on earth" (*Mt* 28:18). In this way, Jesus affirms the perfect fulfillment, in him, of the celebrated prophesy of Daniel concerning the Son of Man. In chapter 7 of his Book, Daniel describes the frightening vision of God who is called "The Ancient of Days", seated on the throne of his heavenly glory (*Dn* 7:9) and then adds: "I saw in the night visions, and behold, with the clouds of heaven there came one like a son of man, and he came to the Ancient of Days and was presented before him. And to him was given dominion and glory and kingdom, that all peoples, nations, and languages should serve him; his dominion is an everlasting dominion, which shall not pass away, and his kingdom one that shall not be destroyed" (*Dn* 7:13-14). This prophecy finds its superabundant fulfillment in the paschal glorification of Jesus in which he receives from the Father royal power and dominion not only on earth but also in heaven. Jesus foretold this glorification during his passion when responding to the High Priest who questioned him concerning his identity: "The Christ the Son of God", Jesus had affirmed. Furthermore, "You will see from now on the Son of Man coming on the clouds of Heaven" (*Mt* 63-64). Daniel had spoken of a Son of Man who would come on the clouds of Heaven.

The vision of Daniel is the final point of a very long biblical tradition, which really begins with the account of the creation of man. Man was created to be the ruler of the earth. God created man and said, "Be fruitful, multiply, fill the earth, subdue it, dominate it" (*Gn* 1:28). Man must be the conqueror of creation. He must be its lord, dependent, naturally, on the great Lord. This initial plan of God was re-expressed more specifically after the fall, firstly, with the vocation of Abraham and the promise of an heir and an inheritance. Abraham lamented and complained to God because he did not have a son. He would not have a true heir: "You have not given me a son", he said to God, "and a domestic or one of my household will be my heir" (*Gn* 15:3). But God promises him a true heir: "One born from you will be your heir" (*Gn* 15:4). He also promises him an inheritance: "To your descendants, I will give this land" (*Gn* 15:18). This first promise of God to Abraham is now re-expressed and extended. While to Abraham was promised the land of Canaan, a limited country, God promises to David, Abraham's descendant, an heir who would be the Lord of the whole earth. The power of this heir, the son of David who would also be the Son of God, would encompass the whole earth: "Ask and I will give you the nations as your inheritance, as your property, the confines of the world" (*Ps* 2:8). With his death and resurrection, Christ, "Son of David, Son of Abraham" *(Mt* 1:1), has been constituted the heir of all things, in which the whole plan of God is achieved. He is, therefore, the omega, the culminating point of human history and of the history of salvation, the definitive word of God, who has established an eternal Covenant. What joy must we feel in contemplating Christ glorified, the universal heir! What confidence must this presence of Christ in our life give to us!

After this first statement, the author makes a second, saying that through the Son, God "also made the world" (*Hb* 9:2). In fact, if he is the *omega*, the final point of history, Christ must also first be the *alpha*, the initial point of everything, the eternal Son, the pre-existing, primordial Word, through whom God has created the world. To the astonished eyes of the Apostles and of the first Christians, Christ's paschal glory fully revealed his own pre-existing glory. Just as the fourth Gospel tells us: "No-one has gone up to Heaven except he who has come down from Heaven" (*Jn* 3:13). No one is able to raise himself to the heights of God except he who had this position from the beginning. The contemplation of the primordial glory of Christ completes the vision of his present glory. Christ is the Word through whom God created the world. In the account of creation, we read: "God said: 'Let there be light' and there was light" (*Gn* 1:3). We now recognize that this created Word is a divine person: the Son of God, through whom God has spoken to us.

After having contemplated the Son as the *omega* and the *alpha*, which he is in his glory as universal heir, the ruler of all, and in his function of creator, the author goes further and contemplates him as he is in himself. He defines him as: "The radiant image of the glory of God and the imprint of his nature" (*Hb* 1:3). We have two extremely dense expressions here, with which the author attempts to define, insofar as is possible, the very being of the Son. The Son is defined according to his relationship with the Father. It is a very strict relationship. The first expression "The radiant image of God's glory" comes from a passage of the Book of Wisdom (*Wis* 7:25-26), but the author reinforces it. The Book of Wisdom was speaking of light, but our present author is referring to glory. This expression emphasizes both the distinction between the two persons of the Father and the Son and their indissolubility, since the radiant image cannot be separated from the source of light. Father and Son therefore have the same nature: they are consubstantial, as was affirmed in later Councils.

In order to reaffirm this union in an even stronger way, the author adds an expression that was not found in the Old Testament; in fact, it was not even found in the New: the Son is "the imprint of the substance" [of God]. In the Book of Wisdom, image and goodness is spoken of: wisdom is an image of the goodness of God. But our present author speaks of the

image vs person

imprint of his substance [translated as "nature"] – two stronger terms. There is separation between the image and the person: an image implies a distance from one who sees the person and tries to reproduce his traits. The imprint however, is produced by direct contact, through which a more faithful representation results. The Son is not a reproduction of God at a distance but a direct expression, not only of his goodness, but of his substance [nature]. The Son is a perfect expression of the very being of the Father. One cannot go beyond this in defining the union of the Son with the Father.

After having defined this relationship, the author returns to the relationship that the Son has with the world and he expresses the ongoing role that he has with respect to creation. This role is a manifestation of power. The Son sustains all things, literally, "with the word of his power". The author is no longer concerned here with creation, but with the conservation of the existence of the universe. Just as God did not have to make some force in order to create the world, since his Word is enough, so also the Son does not need to exhaust himself in maintaining the world in being: the Word of his power is enough. There is a great difference between Christ and the mythological hero, Atlantis (*sic* "Atlas"), of whom Greek mythology speaks,[3] who was represented as one who bore the weight of the world. Christ sustains the whole world with a simple Word.

At this point, the author briefly introduces the decisive stage of salvation, which is the Paschal Mystery of Christ. The Son "when he had made purification for sins, sat down at the right hand of the Majesty on high" (*Hb* 1:3). With these words, the action with which Christ the Priest established the Covenant is described. Two aspects of the Paschal Mystery are indicated: on the one hand, the purification from sins (the priestly function) and on

---

3 Translator's note: According to Greek mythology, for warring against Zeus, Atlas was forced to bear the weight of the heavens upon his shoulders at the edge of the world.

the other hand, the glorification at the right-hand of the Majesty on high. The Son has "made purification for sins"; that is, he has removed the obstacle that impeded the covenant relationship and has established communication by means of that powerful movement of glorification, which has made him pass from this world to the Father by which he has also opened a way for us. Obviously, the greatest obstacle to the covenant is constituted by sin. Therefore, it was indispensable that there be purification from sin. The author does not explain how this purification would be obtained. Neither does he speak of suffering or death because he wants to remain, for the present, in the perspective of glory. He will give this more precisely later on. The glorification is expressed with an image taken from Psalm 109/110: "The Lord said to my Lord: sit at my right-hand, until I make your enemies a footstool for your feet!" In his interrogation before the Sanhedrin, Jesus announced the imminent fulfillment of this oracle: "From now on, you will see the Son of Man seated at the right-hand of the Father" (*Mt* 26:64). The accomplishment of God's design is effected through Christ's Paschal Mystery. By indicating the psalm, as I have just noted, the author prepares his doctrine on the priesthood of Christ, because in the same psalm, there is a second oracle, in the fourth verse, which proclaims: "You are a priest". Christ is the mediator, always working at the right hand of the Majesty on high. He is a mediator who never ceases to communicate to us the intense dynamism of communion that results from his Paschal Mystery.

The author concludes his introduction with a solemn affirmation which prepares the entire following section, which continues to the end of chapter two: Christ seated at the right hand of God is "found to be superior to the angels, the name that he has inherited is more excellent than theirs". What is this name that is "more excellent", or more strictly translated: "very distinct" (διαφορώτερον) from that of the angels?" To define it, it is necessary to read the entire first part; we will do this in the next meditation. This name comprises two main aspects: Christ glorified is the Son of God and our brother. Therefore, he is the perfect mediator. In the final analysis, the name, "High Priest", best expresses the position of Christ glorified and it was precisely this name which God himself proclaimed when he said: "You are a priest forever" (*Ps* 109/110:4; *Hb* 5:6, 10; *Hb* 7:11-28).

3
Christ is the Son of God
and our brother
(Hb 1:5 – 2:16)

We have seen that the author of the Letter to the Hebrews finishes his introduction with an explanation of the name of Christ, which is also a christological explanation. In the first two chapters, the author will provide an exposé of traditional christology based on the texts of the Old Testament in order to prepare the way for a priestly christology. "When he had made purification for sins, he sat down at the right hand of the Majesty on high, having become as much superior to angels as the name he has obtained is more excellent than theirs". In biblical language, the name signifies the dignity of the person and his capacity for relationship. What position has Christ attained on account of his Paschal Mystery?

The author announces that he will explain this by means of a comparison with the angels. What is this comparison? To us it can seem surprising, but at the time of the author, it was indispensable because the angels were considered to be mediators and beings who were always closer to God than us. Furthermore, the angels were considered to have great power over the events of world history because they moved the stars. There is a very close relationship in the Old Testament between the angels and the stars. This comparison with the angels continues to the end of Chapter 2, which indicates that the first part of the Letter, the explanation of traditional christology, is extended to this point (2:18).

The author begins by saying: "For to what angel did God ever say, 'thou art my son, today I have begotten thee?'" This is a rhetorical question that seeks the involvement of the hearers, who would have known exactly where this quote comes from, to whom it was said, and on whose part it was said. They would have known very well that it was a citation from Psalm 2, a messianic and kingly psalm, which is interpreted as messianic precisely because it speaks of the Messiah: it says that the kings of the earth have risen against the Lord and against his Anointed. It is to the Messiah that God says: "Thou art my son, today I have begotten thee". Nothing like this has ever been said to any angel. It is true that in the Old Testament, the angels are sometimes called, "Sons of God" but always in the plural, for example, at the beginning of the Book of Job (*Jb* 1:6; 2:1). In the plural, however, the title simply means a category of celestial beings. God has never said to any special angel: "You are my son, today I have begotten to you". Instead, he said it to Christ. When? The liturgy applies it to the Birth of Christ but the Letter to the Hebrews and St Paul, in a discourse, (*Acts* 13:33), apply it to the resurrection of Christ. At the resurrection of Christ, God said to Christ, "You are my son". As a person, it is clear that Christ has always been the Son of God, because he "...reflects the glory of God and bears the very stamp of his nature" (*Hb* 1:3). However, his human nature did not manifest the form of his filial glory, since, as Son of God, he did not assume the condition of a Son but "of a slave", as St Paul says in his Letter to the Philippians (*Ph* 2:7). Indeed, he took a humble condition, not a glorious one. Only after the passion did Christ assume some manifestation of his filial glory in his human nature. The rhetorical question of the author, issued in a challenging tone, is for us a reason for joy and spiritual boasting. We see our teacher, Jesus, proclaimed Son of God in his human nature and so we can be full of faithfulness, confidence and security.

In the following verse (verse 6) a similar reference is made to the glorification of Christ who has been called first-born, an emphasis taken from Psalm 88/89, where God says of the Son of David: "And I will make him the first-born, the highest of the kings of the earth". The author affirms the fulfillment of this promise in the glorification of Christ. God has introduced Christ as the first-born of the new creation; the author does not use the term κόσμος *"world"* but speaks of the new creation called οἰκουμένη (literally, "the habitated [region]", cf. *Hb* 2:5). This concerns not the birth but the glorification. At that time, it was said: "All the angels of God will adore him". The angels must submit to Christ, because he is not just a man; he is also the Son of God, glorified in his very humanity.

Then, in verse 8, even the title "God" is attributed to Christ. Meanwhile, the Bible says of the angels: "Who makes his angels winds, and his servants flames of fire", leading us to understand that the angels are at the disposition of God for whatever mission is to be completed and indeed they are provisional in the sense that God may need them in one way or another. Instead, it is said of the Son: "Thy throne, O God, is forever and ever". Christ's divinity is proclaimed throughout this quotation of Psalm 44/45. In the original context of the Psalm, this title could not attain its full significance because it was applied in the immediate sense to the King of Israel, God's representative on earth. But when it is applied to the glorified Christ, the title assumes its fullest dimension; we are no longer in the earthly dimension but in the celestial or heavenly dimension. Christ shares God's celestial throne and is truly God from God. The author does not hesitate to proclaim this. In the Gospel of John, Thomas eventually proclaims: "My Lord and my God!" (*Jn* 20:28). Jesus is truly God from God and possesses an Eternal Kingship.

Then the author applies other expressions of this psalm to Christ: "Your royal sceptre is a sceptre of equity, you love righteousness and hate wickedness". Jesus loved justice and hated iniquity because he suffered for our sins. A citation from

Psalm 101/102 enables the author to present yet another aspect of the name of Christ: "Of old thou didst lay the foundation of the earth and the heavens of the work of thy hands". It is the strongest testimony of the whole Bible concerning Christ's collaboration in the work of creation. The author does not hesitate to attribute the world's creation to Christ, the Son of God, and calls him "Lord" in the fuller sense of this title that is attributed to God and here acquires this divine meaning. Christ's dignity consists in the fact that he is the creator of heaven and of earth with God the Father and that he now has the power to effect the final judgment and to destroy the old creation: "They will perish but thou dost endure. They will all wear out like a garment; thou changest them like raiment and they pass away but thou art the same, and thy years have no end". If the angels are powerful in the world because they move the stars, how much more powerful is Christ glorified, he who has the power to bring about an end to the old creation, because he has inaugurated the new creation by means of his resurrection!

Finally, the author again takes up his tone of challenge and question: But to what angel has he ever said, "Sit at my right-hand, until I make thy enemies a stool for thy feet?" Here, the hearers do not hesitate; they recognize the first oracle of Psalm 109/110 which the author has already emphasized in his introduction, in speaking of the Son who is seated at the right hand of the Father. God has never said anything like this to any angel. None of them has ever been invited to sit near God. The angels are always standing, or in a position of service, sent to serve all who must enter into possession of salvation.

So, in the first chapter, the author has presented Christ to us in his relationship with God, a most intimate relationship. Christ is the Son of God in the fullest sense of the word: co-sharing God's throne, he has power over heaven and earth; he is God with God, Lord with Lord. Our hearts can exult with joy as we repeat these glorious texts in prayer.

However, this is only the first aspect of Christ's name. There is another aspect that is no less important for us; in fact, it expresses another difference between Christ and the angels: Christ is our brother. He is presented to us in this way in the second chapter. In verses 6-8, the author cites Psalm 8, which speaks of man's vocation: "What is man that thou art mindful of him, or the Son of Man, that thou carest for him? Thou didst make him for a little while lower than the angels, thou hast crowned him with glory and honour, putting everything in subjection under his feet". Man's vocation, as we have already seen, is that of being the viceroy of the universe. God tells man to fill the earth, to subject it, to dominate it: everything must be subjected to man. The Book of Wisdom specifies how this dominion of man on the earth is to be realized: "With your wisdom, you have formed man, to rule over all the creatures that you have made, to govern the world in holiness and righteousness, and to pronounce justice and uprightness of soul". God's plan for man is this: that man would rule, governing the world with holiness and justice.

The author then makes a reflection on this vocation of man. The text of the Psalm comprises three statements: the affirmation of his having been made lower than the angels, the glorification, and the governorship. Concerning this third point, the author specifies that it concerns a universal rule (v. 8). God has subjected everything to man, "He has left nothing outside his control". The author then observes that this aspect is not yet fully actuated: "As it is, we do not yet see everything in subjection to him". This third aspect is not even realized by Christ: Christ is waiting for his enemies to be made a footstool under his feet. But the author notes that the first two aspects are fully realized in Christ. He suggests that the Psalm is especially applied to Christ, because it is not possible to say that man, in general, may be "made lower than the angels": in order to be made lower, it is first necessary to have been at that same level, so man has not been made lower. Instead, the Son of God has been made lower than the angels, becoming man with men, assuming this humble form of existence.

Then he was crowned with glory and honour, and the author specifies that he was crowned "because he had suffered death". Contemplating the glorified Christ, the author discovers this other aspect of his name. He is the one in whom man's vocation is brought to a fulfillment "so that he might taste death for everyone" (2:9). The man who had been made for a while a little lower than the angels is now crowned with glory and honour because of the suffering of death. We find ourselves in a framework of solidarity: Christ has attained his own glory by means of his complete solidarity with us. He has taken our destiny on himself, which necessarily includes suffering and death as a consequence of sin, and in this way, he has brought our vocation to its fulfillment: that of being crowned with glory and honour.

The author states: "For it was fitting that he for whom and by whom all things exist, in bringing many sons to glory, should make the pioneer of their salvation perfect through suffering". Christ, the pioneer, who leads us to salvation, has been made perfect by means of suffering. In order to sanctify us, he has placed himself in solidarity with us by becoming one with us. The author then announces: "That is why he is not ashamed to call them brethren, saying, 'I will proclaim thy name to my brethren, in the midst of the congregation, I will praise thee'". This citation is taken from Psalm 21/22, the Psalm of the passion: "My God, my God, why hast thou forsaken me" (v. 1; *Mt* 27:46). This is a psalm of supplication, pronounced in a situation of extreme anguish, but it is also understood to be a promise of a sacrifice and thanksgiving after liberation: "I will tell of thy name to my brethren". That is to say: I will render you thanks in the midst of my brothers, in the midst of the assembly, I will sing your praises (*Hb* 2:12). Christ, in his passion, has fulfilled this psalm, he has explicitly promised to announce the name of God to his brothers after his victory over death; he now fulfills this promise after his glorification. His present activity consists in announcing to us the name of God who is good, telling us about his mercy, telling us that his mercy is eternal. Christ recognizes us as his brothers. The Son of God and our Brother are two aspects of the name of Christ, aspects that render him more distinct from the angels: more united to God, more united to us. The angels are intermediaries between the two.

Christ has a "universal" mediation, which has descended to the lowest level of human misery, namely: being condemned to death. For this reason, he was exulted to the heights of celestial glory, to God's right hand. This is truly what is so mind-blowing about Christian revelation: that the Son of God descended to the lowest level of our misery and on this account, was raised in his human nature to the highest level of divine glory. The glory of Christ is not the glory of an ambitious individual who is satisfied with his own exploits; nor is it the glory of a warrior who has conquered his enemies by the power of his arm. Rather, it is the glory of love, the glory of having loved to the end and of having reestablished the communion between us sinners and his Father. By means of his filial docility to his Father and his fraternal solidarity with us, even to the point of death, Christ has become the perfect Mediator; he has become High Priest of the New Covenant. This exposition of traditional Christology focuses in this way on an affirmation of Christ's priesthood. Christ has become "a merciful and faithful High Priest in the service of God" (*Hb* 2:17). This contemplation infuses joy and confidence into us because we have more than an advocate; we have a brother who intercedes for us, a brother who has promised to announce to us, following his glorification, the name of the Father, and who announces it now. He is a brother who does not forget us in his glory, because his own glory is truly the fruit of his solidarity with us. Let us give thanks to Our Lord for this revelation that is so beautiful and so consoling. Let us ask him for the grace to adore him, the Son of God, who is God with God,

Lord with Lord. Finally, let us have full confidence in him, our brother.

4
How Christ has become High Priest
(Hb 2:17-18)

We saw earlier that, in the first part of his homily, the author of the Letter to the Hebrews demonstrates that the name inherited by Christ, by virtue of his Paschal Mystery, contains two principal aspects: Christ the Son of God and Christ our brother. His is a more excellent name than that of the angels because Christ is more united to the Father and more united to us. It is the name of the perfect mediator. It is the name of a High Priest. At the end of chapter 2, in verse 17, the author declares: "Therefore, he had to be made like his brethren in every respect, so that he might become a merciful and faithful High Priest in the service of God".

In this text, the author effects two surprising innovations, which we must consider so as to have a proper concept of the sacrifice and priesthood of Christ and a correct notion of our participation in this priesthood. The first innovation consists in applying to Christ the title of High Priest; the second consists in a new way of being High Priest.

The affirmation of Christ's priesthood was indeed a great novelty. By now we are used to speaking of the priesthood of Christ. It seems obvious to us. We have no problem with it. However, if we examine the texts of the New Testament, we can see that the issue was not clear at all for the first Christians. Prior to the Letter to the Hebrews, there is no text that attributes the title of Priest or High Priest to Jesus. In the Gospels, many titles are given to Jesus: teacher, prophet, Son of David, Son of Man, Son of God, but never the title of Priest. The Gospel tradition uses this title only for the levitical priesthood and, for the most part, in a context that is in stark contraposition to Christ! The High Priests, in particular, are presented as hostile to Jesus. St Paul never uses the title of High Priest: neither for Jesus nor for anyone else.

It is a situation that is easily understood because the first Christian perspective did not perceive any relationship between Jesus' existence and the institution of the priesthood, such as existed in the Old Testament. The person of Jesus was not presented as a priest, according to the sacerdotal concept then in vogue, and this for the simple reason that Jesus had not come from the tribe of Levi. According to the Law of Moses, only members of the tribe of Levi could assume priesthood. Jesus belonged to the tribe of Judah and could not, therefore, be a priest according to the law. During his life, he never claimed to be a priest. He never exercised any priestly, ritual function. His ministry was of a prophetic and sapiential nature, not a priestly one. The "priest" was a man of the sanctuary, a man of ritual sacrifice and of the entire system of ritual purity. Jesus never entered the sanctuary; he entered into the courts of the Temple, but never into the building of the sanctuary. He never offered a ritual sacrifice and he gave no importance to ritual purity.

In the preaching of the prophets, there is often a strong polemic against the ritual worship of the priests: for example, in chapter 1 of the prophet Isaiah, we read: "What to me is the multitude of your sacrifices says the Lord: I have had enough of burnt offerings of rams and of the fat of fed beasts; I do not delight in the blood of bulls, or of lambs or he-goats. Bring no more vain offerings" (*Is* 1:11,13). This is a strong polemic. In a certain way, Jesus continued this prophetic tradition. The Gospels refer to a systematic action of Jesus against the ritual notion of religion. Insistently, with his words and actions, Jesus fought against the ancient notion of sanctification by ritual separations; this was the concept of the Old Testament, which could contribute nothing more. In a controversy concerning ritual purity, Jesus demonstrated that true religion does not consist in rites of separation (consecration). Ritual purity seemed to have enormous importance because it conditioned participation in worship. Jesus denied this importance. Speaking against the ritual observations around food, its preparation and eating, he said: "There is nothing outside of man which by going into him can defile him" (*Mk* 7:15). The evangelist observes: "Thus he declared all foods clean" (*Mk* 7:19) and eliminated preoccupations with ritual purity. In the same vein, Jesus' initiatives contrasted with Sabbath observance. There are numerous examples of this in all four Gospels. In the Gospel of St Matthew, Jesus quotes a divine declaration that is very significant for a new concept of priesthood. In the Book of the prophet Hosea, God declares: "I desire steadfast love and not sacrifice, the knowledge of God rather than burnt offerings" (*Ho* 6:6). Between the two possible ways of serving God: one with rites of immolation of animal sacrifices; the other in human relationships, Jesus decidedly chose the second, knowing that God prefers mercy to ritual sacrifices and has a preference for personal relationships. Therefore, nothing in the person of Jesus, either in his activities or in his teaching, gives a sense of the ancient priesthood.

But what can be said about his death? Is it not necessary perhaps to admit that everything becomes sacrificial and therefore sacerdotal. Our response now is in the affirmative, of course. However, at the time of Jesus, the response was negative. The sacrificial character of Jesus' death could not be perceived by the old mentality. Indeed, the event of Calvary was none other than a sacrificial ritual but it was presented as the opposite. It seemed the exact opposite of a sacrificial ritual because it was a legal penalty, the execution of one who had been condemned to death. A legal penalty is the precise inverse of a sacrifice. As a result, the absence of sacrificial and sacerdotal vocabulary in the Gospels and in the first writings of the New Testament is a well-known phenomenon.

In spite of this situation, the Letter to the Hebrews proclaims that Christ is a priest; indeed, he is a High Priest, the true, unique High Priest. How is this innovation justified, which then leads to other innovations and, in particular, to the priestly notion of the Christian life and ministry? The innovation of the Letter to the Hebrews is justified as a further deepening in the mystery of Christ in the light of the scriptures. As an event, the mystery of Christ accomplished its fullness with his passion, glorification and gift of the Holy Spirit. Its interpretation, however, would have to develop little by little. The Apostles had received an overall revelation; they understood that the scriptures were fulfilled in Christ. A progressive elaboration was required in this overall revelation, which would gradually explain all the dimensions of the salvific event. It would have to carry out an "inventory" of the richness of Christ.

The author of the Letter to the Hebrews discovered in Psalm 109/110 the priestly aspect of the mystery of Christ, which he could not miss, since among the various traditions of the Old Testament, it cannot be denied that the priestly tradition held the most important position. The priesthood is certainly one of the principal aspects of the biblical revelation. This to be expected because Israel's vocation was to be the people of God and the function of the priesthood was precisely that of securing the relationship of the people with God. This importance is reflected in the Pentateuch, which dedicates long chapters to the organization of priestly worship and describes the consecration of the High Priest in many details. In the historical books, one can see that the entire history of the chosen people involves an ever-increasing concentration on two institutions: the Davidic dynasty on the one hand and the priesthood of Jerusalem on the other.

After the return from exile, the emphasis develops into an eschatological expectation of a priestly Messiah. This expectation was attested to in a very explicit way in the documents of Qumran where there are even some texts that speak of two Messiahs of "two anointed ones": one would be regal or kingly, the other priestly. In the rule of the Qumran Congregation, it is written: "They will be governed by the first laws until the prophet and the Messiah of Aaron and Israel come". The Messiah of Aaron is the priestly Messiah. The Messiah of Israel is the Davidic Messiah. In other documents (not of Qumran) called the "Testaments of the Twelve Patriarchs", the same expectation is expressed. A document called "From Damascus" has it in the singular with the two names: the Messiah of Israel and of Aaron. In that environment, it seems that they were awaiting a single person with a double messianic dignity: one priestly; the other kingly. This expectation was normal because the final fulfillment would indeed have to be a fulfillment of all the important aspects of God's plan and the priestly aspect was essential; it could not be missing.

This expectation posed a difficult question for the Christians: "How to respond to the mystery of Christ? What aspect of this priestly expectation can be recognized in the mystery of Christ? At first sight, as I said, the response seemed to be negative but the author of the Letter to the Hebrews discovers in the Psalms the oracle that affirmed the priesthood of the Messiah (Ps 109/110:4). He would therefore make a profound reflection which would bring him to recognize that the priestly aspect was indeed present in the mystery of Christ. Furthermore, Christ was the only perfect priest. The fulfillment of scripture had occurred in an unforeseen and disconcerting manner, as often happens.

The application to Christ of the title of priest produced a deepening concept of priesthood. This is something that we must welcome. The constant temptation is to return to the Old Testament, because the Old Testament concept corresponds to

nah.
it's a revealed
religion

spontaneous religiosity. Christian faith, however, is something new and distinct. According to the Letter to the Hebrews, Christ's manner of becoming High Priest was completely new: "Therefore he had to be made like his brethren in every respect so that he might become a merciful and faithful High Priest" (*Hb* 2:17). This is truly amazing! It is precisely contrary to the whole Old Testament biblical tradition because, far from speaking of assimilation or likeness, the witness of the Old Testament underlines and emphasizes the need for separation, that is, a ritual separation in view of sanctification. To enter into contact with sacred realities, the Levites were set apart; they did not have an inheritance among the sons of Israel (*Dt* 18:1-2); even their census was conducted separately (*Nb* 1:47). For Aaron and his sons, the separation was even more marked and more insistent by means of the rites of consecration, especially the immolation of great quantities of animals (*Lv* 8) and with many, severe precepts of ritual purity (*Lv* 21). So, the ancient High Priest appeared to be elevated above common mortals. The first word that Sirach uses when speaking of Aaron is indeed the word "to elevate": 'He elevated Aaron' (*Sir* 45:6). The subject is God, so then, God elevated Aaron. The priesthood set him apart. Sirach never tires of describing the splendor of the priest when he speaks of Aaron and then again when he speaks of Simon, the High Priest, son of Onias, in his own time. He uses all the celestial or heavenly similes: the sun, the moon, the stars and the rainbow (*Sir* 50:5-7). The priest finds himself in the celestial zones. Since the time of the Exodus, this dignity roused ambitions and jealousies. Let us remember the episode of Korah the son of Izhar, and his accomplices, who wanted to take the priesthood for themselves (*Nb* 16). In the centuries that followed the exile, even more aggressive rivalries occurred, because political and priestly authority was joined together. The Second Book of the Maccabees makes dreadful references to these in chapter 4: corruption, political manipulation and manoeuvering, homicidal treachery *et cetera*, are all mentioned. Similarly, the Qumran documents also express criticism of the godless high priesthood.

Based on this historical context, the statement of the Letter to the Hebrews signifies a complete contrast. It is directly opposed to the mentality and conduct of the contemporary High Priests. In their eyes, the Pontificate constituted the highest of all promotions and they looked for the most politically effective means to attain it, even if these were dishonest. Christ is orientated in precisely the opposite direction. In becoming High Priest, Jesus renounced every privilege and instead of holding himself above all the others, he made himself like them in every way, as a brother, and he accepted treachery and humiliation in his passion and death. Instead of a higher position between man and God, Christ took the lowest position: a complete solidarity with the least of men, that is, with those condemned to death. It seems clear that when the author tells us that Christ made himself completely like his brothers, he is thinking especially of this: not only of the Incarnation which he had spoken of earlier but, above all, of his suffering unto death. In the following verse (18), he immediately asserts, "Because he [Christ] himself has suffered and been tempted, he has been able to help those who are tempted".

This attitude was not only opposed to the abuses deplored by the author of the Book of the Maccabees; it also went against the traditional ideas of the most religious Jews. These had great zeal for the holiness of the priesthood. They aimed to maintain the ritual separations. To require of the High Priest a complete similarity with other members or the people seemed to them incompatible with a correct concept of priesthood. In particular, contact with death was absolutely prohibited to the High Priest since it was conceived that there was an incompatibility between the corruption of death and the holiness of God. The High Priest did not have the right to mourn for anyone, not even for his mother or father (*Lv* 21:11), because that would have meant contact with death. Jesus, instead, has become High Priest by means of his own suffering and death, offering it with filial obedience and fraternal solidarity. Clearly, his meditation on the mystery of Christ, that is, on the mystery of the Passion and of the Pasch, has led the author of the Letter to the Hebrews to turn away from the former perspectives, insisting on the need for human solidarity and abandoning the idea of ritual separation in the Paschal Mystery of Christ. Christ's complete acceptance of human solidarity effectively achieved what the old rites of priestly consecration, by means of separation, sought in vain to obtain, namely: the elevation of man to intimacy with God and the union of human nature with the divine. This mystery has great importance for priestly consecration. The glory of the risen Christ continues to be recognized as the glory of the priesthood.

The author had expressed in verse 9 that Jesus is now crowned with glory and honour because of the suffering of death. That is, Jesus has been admitted, with his human nature, to intimacy with God. Instead of through legal separations, his elevation to intimacy with God was achieved through his acceptance of a complete sharing in his brothers' destiny. This acceptance was, at the same time, an act of priestly mercy. The generous attitude of Jesus, the Mediator, led him to fully welcome human solidarity. Human suffering existed: death, sin. They are a human reality. Jesus has descended into the depths of this human misery, infused divine love into it and traced a way out for us, that is: a way of salvation. He has made suffering and death an occasion of extreme love. In this way, he became High Priest. He has traced out the way of the New Covenant that is the way of communion with God, regained for us sinners.

All this is, indeed, extraordinarily beautiful. In prayer, you can contemplate this admirable love of God: Jesus "had to be made like his brethren in every respect, so that he might become a merciful and faithful High Priest in the service of God". He has accepted humiliation, suffering and death with immense generosity. We must understand our participation in his priesthood in this way. We must become profoundly at one with our brothers, taking on ourselves their joys and sufferings, their fatigues and hopes, their anxieties and aspirations so as to manifest to them the love of God and to bring them to divine communion.

It seems appropriate to me to make a final observation on the rites. The sacramental rites of episcopal consecration and priestly ordination have a significance and efficacy that is radically different from equivalent rites of the Old Testament because they are set in relation to the priestly consecration of Christ which was brought about by means of filial obedience and fraternal solidarity. The Old Testament rites had none of this efficacy or meaning. We have to be aware of the profound change. The rites are always necessary, in a certain sense, but we must see what their efficacy is: do they set apart for relationship or do they just set apart? The dynamism of communion and love, which is established in the heart of Jesus by the Holy Spirit, is also offered to our hearts so that we may be true ministers of the New Covenant. Open yourselves, therefore, to this revelation of a new way of understanding the priesthood and ask for the grace to be docile to its intense dynamism.

5
Christ: High Priest, worthy of faith
(Hb 3:1-4, 14)

When, for the first time, at the end of Chapter 2, the author of the Letter to the Hebrews speaks of Christ as Ἀρχιερεύς, *Archiereus,* High Priest, he annexes two qualifications to this title: "merciful and worthy of faith".[4] Christ "had to be made like his brethren in every respect, so that he might become a merciful and faithful high priest in the service of God" (2:17 *RSV*). You can see that these adjectives do not express individual virtues such as, for example, courage, patience or prudence; rather they concern relationships between persons and for that reason, they truly designate two priestly qualities, that is, two indispensable qualities for exercising priestly mediation. They are also indispensable qualities for exercising pastoral ministry. They correspond to the two dimensions of the mediation of the covenant: "worthy of faith" concerns the capacity for placing the people in relationship with God, as the author explicitly says, "worthy of faith for relations/dealings with God" ("degno di fede per i rapporti con Dio" – Italian Episcopal Conference Translation). "Merciful" expresses the capacity for understanding and offering fraternal assistance to others. These two qualities must necessarily be present together in order to make a priest. A man who is full of compassion for the brethren, but who is not accredited to approach God, could not exercise

---

4 Translator's note: For Hebrews 2:17, I have departed from the RSV translation of the Greek πιστος as simply *faithful,* in favour of the Italian Episcopal Conference *Revised* Translation (CEI 2008), *worthy of faith* for the reason provided in the text by the Author.

priestly mediation so as to establish the covenant. From the religious point of view, his compassion would be sterile; it would be merely philanthropic; it would remain at the earthly level. In the opposite case, one who is accredited to be near God but lacks the bond of solidarity with us could not be our High Priest either. His self-centred position would not be to our advantage. The union of these two capacities for relationship is fundamental for the priesthood of the New Covenant.

In Christ, such a union is perfectly secured because, by his passion, he has joined to his filial glory what he fulfils in us through his solidarity. We who participate in the priesthood of Christ must have these two qualities, these two capacities for relating.

At the beginning of the next chapter, the author takes up again the second adjective: "worthy of faith". He says: "Brethren, who share in a heavenly call, consider Jesus, the apostle and high priest of our confession. He was faithful to him who appointed him, just as Moses also was faithful in God's house" (3:1-2). In these verses, the Greek adjective «πιστος» is not translated "worthy of faith", but "faithful". The first edition of the New Testament of the Italian Episcopal Conference had put "faithful, fedele". The new edition corrected this and put "worthy of faith". This is a better translation, because "worthy of faith" is the first meaning of the Greek adjective adopted by the author and it is this meaning that is required by this context. Faithful ("fedele") is a derived meaning, possible in other contexts, but it does not fit well in this one. When it is translated as "faithful", the verb is put in the past tense: consider Jesus who has been made faithful in his Passion. In the Greek phrase however, we find the present participle: the author does not invite us to contemplate Jesus as he was in the past, but as he is now, Christ glorified, who is fully revealed to be worthy of faith, trustworthy, authoritative. With his resurrection, God has presented him to all as worthy of faith, as St Paul says at the end of his discourse in the Areopagus (*Acts* 17:31). We are not concerned here with the faithfulness of Jesus before God, a quality that Jesus fully possesses; this is not in doubt. Here, we are interested in a quality that he possesses now in glory.

Indeed, in order to make his thought more clear, the author introduces a comparison with Moses, referring to an episode of the Book of Numbers, chapter 12, in which the concern is not so much Moses' faithfulness, which had been imperfect (cf. *Dt* 32:50-51), but with a problem of authority. Miriam and Aaron spoke against Moses, saying: "Has the Lord only spoken through Moses? Has he not also spoken through us?" (*Nb* 12:1-2). As you can see, Miriam and Aaron were contesting the authority of their brother and his privileged role as mediator of God's Word. The Lord heard this challenge and responded firmly: "Hear my words: If there is a prophet among you, I the LORD make myself known to him in a vision, I speak with him in a dream. Not so with my servant Moses; he is entrusted with all my house" (*Nb* 12:6-7). The author of the Letter to the Hebrews has recovered this expression. The challenge is punished: "The anger of the Lord came against them... and behold Miriam was leprous, white as snow" (*Nb* 12:9,10). Miriam was punished because she had contested the authority of her brother as the privileged messenger of the Word of God. To be saved from her leprosy, she would have to seek his intercession and his authority.

In this phrase, (*Hb* 3:2), as regards Moses, the reference is to the Book of Numbers; as regards Jesus, the reference is to the oracle given to King David through the prophet Nathan. At the end of this oracle, God speaks to the Messiah who is the Son of David and the Son of God: "I will confirm him [alternate translation: "make him worthy of faith"] in my house and in my kingdom" (*1 Ch* 17:14 LXX). The author has given this argument from scripture to confirm that Jesus is "worthy of faith". In his public life, Jesus showed himself to be authoritative, to be "worthy of faith". The Gospels relate: "he taught them as one who had authority, and not as the scribes" (*Mk* 1:22). His authority is fully revealed in the antithesis of the discourse of the sermon on the mount: "You have heard that it was said ... but I say to you ..." (*Mt* 5:21-22, 27-28, 31-32, 33-34, 38-39, 43-44). This authority found its perfect fulfillment in the moment of the resurrection, when he brought it to an unsurpassed perfection. God presented Christ risen as worthy of faith for all those who have a relationship with him. Let us receive with joy, this divine revelation; let us receive Christ our High Priest who is worthy of faith, so as to enter into relationship with God.

After having spoken in this way about Jesus, the High Priest, worthy of faith, the author confirms this quality by attributing to Jesus the qualification of a builder of the house. This qualification had not been given to Moses who had not constructed a house for God, but only a tent and a modest tent at that. The Son of David would be the builder of God's house. According to the oracle of Nathan to whom God spoke: "He shall build a house for my name" (*1 Sam* 7:13; *1 Ch* 17:12). The builder is Christ. To the Jews who wanted proof of his authority after the cleansing of the Temple, Jesus responded: "Destroy this Temple and in three days, I will raise it up (*Jn* 2:19). The evangelist explains: "He spoke of the Temple of his body (*Jn* 2:21). The author then says: "Yet Jesus has been counted worthy of as much more glory than Moses as the builder of a house has more honour than the house" (*Hb* 3:3). By his passion and resurrection, Christ has built God's house. The author then adds another argument and makes a comparison, saying that while Moses was said to be "... worthy of faith in all God's house, as a servant", Christ is worthy "as a Son over all God's house". Moses was called, "Servant" (θεράπων) of God, not a "slave" (δουλος). "Servant" is a higher title. Christ, however, has a title that is higher still: He is "Son" forever according to the oracle of Nathan (*2 S* 7:14; *1 Ch* 17:13) and confirmed by the Gospels (*Mt* 3:17; 17:5ff). As Son, he has authority over the house.

You see with what insistence the author presents this first priestly quality of Christ: that of being worthy of faith, authoritative, and trustworthy for dealings with God. We who participate in Christ's priesthood must have this quality above all: to be worthy of faith for dealings with God. Indeed, we can ask ourselves if that is truly what we are. What is the condition for being truly worthy of faith for dealings with God? The condition is that of being full of faith in Christ. He who is full of faith in Christ participates in the authority of Christ himself.

The author then continues his preaching with a long exhortation that puts us on guard against the lack of faith or even its absence: «απιστια». After having said, "We are his house if we hold fast our confidence and pride in our hope" (*Hb* 3:6), the author continues: "Therefore, as the Holy Spirit says, "Today, when you hear his voice, do not harden your hearts as in the rebellion, on the day of testing in the wilderness"" (*Hb* 3:7). This is a quote from Psalm 94/95, which also serves as an *invitatory verse* in the Liturgy of the Hours. In the Old Testament, the voice of which this psalm speaks is the voice of God: "Today, when you hear his voice". However, in the context of the Letter to the Hebrews, the voice is Christ's: "Today, when you hear his voice", because now the voice of God is achieved through Christ's voice. God's words are communicated to us through Christ and we must put our faith in him, receiving his words and his ministry with faith so that we also may become worthy of faith for dealings with God.

In the Hebraic text of the psalm, various episodes of the history of the Exodus are highlighted. Among them, two places are named, Massah and Meribah, and there is also reference to another episode of a divine oath recounted in the Book of Numbers: "Therefore I swore in my anger that they should not enter my rest" (*Ps* 94/95; 11; cf. *Nb* 14:21-23). In the Greek text which is naturally the one that is cited in the Letter to the Hebrews, reference is only made to this third episode because the two names, Massah and Meribah, have been translated as proper nouns, which in reality they are: that is two proper nouns given to two places in the Bible. Perhaps we too easily forget this important episode recounted in the Book of Numbers, immediately following the challenge against Moses. Let us rest awhile with the idea that they were bound to traverse the desert for forty years. The Books of Numbers and Deuteronomy tell us that after having escaped from Egypt and being for a brief time in the desert of Sinai, the Israelites were invited by God to enter the Promised Land immediately. God says, "You have stayed long enough at this mountain; turn and take your journey, and go to the hill country of the Amorites... Behold, I have set the land before you; go in and take possession of the land which the Lord swore to your fathers" (*Dt* 1:6-8). Deuteronomy specifies that from Mt Sinai to Kadesh-barnea, which is found on the border of the Promised Land, is just eleven days' journey (*Dt* 1:2), not forty years.

The people request that they might first mandate some men to explore this country that was still unknown to them; the proposal was accepted: twelve men were mandated, one for each tribe, and Moses gave precise instructions to them (*Nb* 13:17-20). Upon returning from their explorations, the twelve men give two contrasting reports. The first is very positive: "We came to the land to which you sent us; it flows with milk and honey, and this is its fruit" (*Nb* 13:27). At this point, the men showed a cluster of grapes of such enormous dimensions that it required two men to carry it between them (*Nb* 13:23). This cluster of grapes becomes the symbol of the Promised Land. Even now, it is still found on the coins and stamps of Israel. The other report is less enthusiastic and begins with a "but": "Yet the people who dwell in the land are strong, and the cities are fortified and very large; and besides, we saw the descendants of Anak there" (*Nb* 13:28).

Following these two contrasting reports, two possible but different attitudes are found. The first is the attitude of faith, which concentrates on the word of the Lord who had said to them: Enter. Take possession. It is the attitude suggested by Moses who says to the people: "Do not be in dread or afraid them. The Lord your God who goes before you, will himself fight for you, just as he did in Egypt before your eyes" (*Dt* 1:29-30). If faith is maintained on the strength of God's Word, on his faithfulness to his promise, if they continue with courage, if they face all situations, knowing themselves to be always helped by the Lord, then, "All things are possible to him who believes" (*Mk* 9:23), because he has God's help.

The other position, however, is not centred on the Word of God but on the difficulties of the task at hand. The people of the country are powerful and the cities are fortified. We know from psychology that when we fix our attention only on the difficulties, they become gigantic and insurmountable. This is what happened to the Israelites at this time. They said: "Whither are we going up? Our brethren have made our hearts melt, saying, 'the people are greater and taller than we; the cities are great and fortified up to heaven; and moreover we have seen the sons of Anakim'" (*Dt* 1:28). Their attention is focused on the difficulties and these become overwhelming: How can we besiege and assail cities fortified to the heavens? This sows doubt concerning the Lord's good intentions. They say: "Because the Lord hated us, he has brought us forth out of the land of Egypt, to give us into the hands of the Amorites, to destroy us" (*Dt* 1:27). They attribute a hostile intention to God, a plan of destruction rather than of love.

This attitude of the people naturally offends the Lord because it is opposed to his gentle love, and the Lord demands: "How long will this people despise me? And how long will they not believe in me, in spite of all the signs which I have wrought among them?" (*Nb* 14:11). So God swears the oath which is recorded in the Psalm: "but truly, as I live, and as all the earth shall be filled with the glory of the LORD, none of the men who have seen my glory and my signs which I wrought in Egypt and in the wilderness, and yet have put me to the proof these ten times and have not hearkened to my voice, shall see the land which I swore to give to their fathers; and none of those who despised me shall see it" (*Nb* 14:20-23). God decides that the whole people would wander for forty years through the desert until the generation of adults who had rebelled had died. Only the new generation, formed of the children who had not taken part in the rebellion, were led to Promised Land (*Dt* 1:39).

The author of the Letter to the Hebrews draws this episode to our attention so as to compare it to our situation as Christians. It is not a comparison with the situation of those Israelites who wandered for forty years in the desert, but with those who found themselves at the frontiers of the Promised Land. The forty years in the desert are for those who do not believe. We, however, find ourselves at the frontier of the Promised Land and we hear ourselves called to proclaim this good news of the Gospel: "The Kingdom of God is at hand" (*Mk* 1:15); the Kingdom of God is here and we are invited to enter it immediately. "Let us, therefore, strive to enter" (*Hb* 4:11), says the author, who explains: "For we who have believed enter that rest" (*Hb* 4:3). The Lord invites us to enter into his kingdom to gather the fruits of the Spirit which are much more beautiful than the fruit of the legendary cluster of grapes. The fruits of the Spirit, Saint Pauls says, are love, joy and peace (*Gal* 5:22). The Lord invites us to live the beatitudes proclaimed by him: "Blessed are the poor in spirit, for theirs is the Kingdom of Heaven. Blessed are the merciful... the pure of heart... the peacemakers" (Cf. *Mt* 5:3-9).

Obviously we will encounter difficulties, dangers and obstacles, to the degree that we will often be tempted to lose faith and to turn back. Difficulties will not be lacking but they need not constitute a reason for discouragement. So we must, above all, proclaim our faith, as St Paul did in such a daring tone in the Letter to the Romans. St Paul asked: "Who shall separate us from the love of Christ?" He then selects all the most tremendous obstacles: "Shall tribulation, or distress, or persecution, or famine, or nakedness, or peril, or the sword?" He responds: "In all these things, we are more than conquerors through him who loved us (*Rm* 8:35-37). St Paul coins a new Greek verb: "ὑπερνικῶμεν", "more than conquerors" (*RSV Rom* 8:37), "We conquer overwhelmingly" (*NAB Rm* 8:37), to proclaim this superabundant victory. This is the reaction of faith before circumstances that pose obstacles to our spiritual life and to our apostolate. We must have the heart of a conqueror, and even more so. It all depends on the attitude that we assume. So let us truly believe in the Word of the Lord who tells us to enter without delay into his Kingdom and to help others to enter. Let us go forward with the Lord's help so that we may be worthy of relationship with God, because we are full of faith. Otherwise, we allow ourselves to be overcome by difficulties and by obstacles that we encounter. We magnify them and, as a result, our lives become sad and sterile. We are no longer worthy of faith because we lack faith; the lack of faith is a radical sin which lies at the root of so many other sins. The author of the Letter to the Hebrews puts us on guard against it: "Take care brethren, lest there be in any of you an evil, unbelieving heart, leading you to fall away from the living God" (*Hb* 3:12).

During the Spiritual Exercises, we must ask ourselves if we truly have an attitude of faith in all circumstances, a faith that corresponds to the Lord's promises and his gifts. We must ask the Lord to purify our hearts of any lack of faith, so that we can be worthy of faith, in our ministry, for dealings with God.

In the episode of the Book of Numbers, the gravest fault was that of those who had taught others to distrust. The text refers to the men that Moses had sent to explore the country and who had, upon their return, murmured in the community, setting it against him by discrediting the Promised Land. These men died. They were stricken by a plague before the Lord (*Nb* 14:36-37). Punishment was immediate for them. For the others, their punishment was a long march in the desert. The instigators of the rebellion were punished immediately because their fault had been graver than that of the others.

We must seriously ask ourselves if perhaps we have spread criticisms, irritability or pessimism to those around us. Let us also ask ourselves if we may have at times provoked discouragement in those around us by drawing attention to the difficulties, to the negative side of a situation that may really exist. We must insist on the positive side of things; not on what is lacking. We must listen to Jesus who tells us: "In the world, you will have tribulation" (*Jn* 16:33). We must be full of faith so as to participate in Christ's victory over the world and, in this way, walk with supernatural optimism to become worthy of faith for dealings with God.

6
Christ, Merciful High Priest
(Hb 4:15-16)

Having now meditated on the first priestly quality of Christ, that is, his absolute trustworthiness and authority, let us now meditate on another priestly quality, described at the end of chapter 2, with some insistence, but explained later on.

In chapter 4, verse 14, the author concludes his contemplation of the glorified Christ who is High Priest and worthy of faith in this way: "Since then, we have a great High Priest who has passed through the heavens, Jesus, the Son of God, let us hold fast our confession". Jesus is the Son of God, glorified, fully worthy of faith. Therefore, we must have faith in him. In the following verse, the author moves on to treat of another priestly quality: "For we have not a High Priest who is unable to sympathize with our weaknesses, but one who in every respect has been tempted as we are, yet without sin". This declaration is followed by a brief but very encouraging exhortation: "Let us then with confidence draw near to the throne of grace, that we may receive mercy and find grace to help in time of need". The author enables us to see that the two priestly qualities in Christ complement each other also from our point of view. Christ who is worthy of faith has guided us to the adhesion of faith. Christ who is merciful has fully awakened our faithfulness. If he was only a glorified High Priest in heaven, perhaps we would not draw near to him, finding him too distant from our weakness; perhaps we would doubt his capacity to understand or to sympathize with us. However, there is this other aspect that removes the strength of any objections: Christ is authoritative, worthy of faith for dealings with God, but he is also the merciful priest, full of compassion for us sinners, and wanting to help us. In our priestly ministry, we must unite the two qualities: authority and mercy, authority and understanding.

The author presents the mercy of Christ as a sentiment that is profoundly imbued with humanity: it is compassion towards his own, acquired by sharing in their fate. So it is not just a superficial sentiment of one who is easily and emotionally moved. Rather it concerns a capacity acquired through personal experience of suffering. The author helps us to understand that to be able to pity, it is necessary to have suffered personally. One must have passed through the same tests and the same sufferings as those he wants to help. Christ can have pity because he has been tested in all things, just like us. From his birth he knew poverty and exclusion; he knew hunger, thirst, tiredness, contradiction, hostility, betrayal, unjust condemnation and even the cross. In this way, he acquired an extraordinary capacity for compassionate understanding.

God's mercy had already been manifested in the Old Testament in a number of very moving ways. However, they lacked one dimension: they were not expressed with a human heart nor acquired through suffering experiences in human existence. Christ has given God's mercy this new dimension, which is so touching and so comforting for us.

In this regard, we can note a strong contrast with some of the ancient priestly traditions. Indeed, some texts of the Old Testament require, on the part of the priest, not mercy, but severity in dealing with sinners. The Old Testament did not yet fully have the concept of priesthood as mediation, considering it bound almost exclusively to the idea of worship. It was preoccupied with the priest's relationship with God. To emphasize that God had set the priest apart, it was necessary that he be decisively opposed to sinners who were God's enemies. It seems quite logical at first sight. According to this point of view, it is not possible to be at

But
EBK
a
priest...

the same time for God and for his enemies.

This is the teaching that has come down to us through the Book of Exodus as characteristic of the institution of the levitical priesthood: the people have abandoned themselves to the idolatry of the Golden Calf. Having descended from Sinai, Moses calls out to ask who is for God. The Levites come to carry out his orders: "Thus says the Lord, God of Israel, 'Put every man his sword on his side, and go to and fro from gate to gate throughout the camp, and slay every man his brother, and every man his companion, and every man his neighbour'" (*Ex* 32:27). This is a ruthless order. The Levites carry it out and slay about 3,000 persons. As a result, Moses declares that they have obtained the priesthood: "Today you have ordained yourselves for the service of the Lord, each one at the cost of his son and of his brother, that he may bestow a blessing upon you this day" (*Ex* 32:29).

Another episode, no less crude, is recounted in chapter 25 of the Book of Numbers. This episode concerns Phinehas, a Levite, who had surprised an Israelite who was sinning with a Midianite woman in his tent, in an idolatrous context: his response was to kill them both with a single thrust of his lance. In this way, he obtained the promise of perpetual priesthood for himself and his family (*Nb* 25:6-12).

From this episode, we can understand the contrast of the priesthood of Christ which is the priesthood of the New Covenant. Far from demanding a ruthless severity against sinners, he requires boundless mercy. Christ has not become a priest who rages against us sinners; on the contrary, by sharing our miserable fate, which is the consequence of our sins, he has acquired priestly mercy.

This change of perspective was first manifested in his passions during his public life. Jesus received sinners and accepted the invitation to eat with them, to the degree that he was called, ironically, a "friend of publicans and sinners (*Mt* 11:19; *Lk* 7:34). To his critics who held this behaviour against him, he responded vehemently: "Go and learn what this means, 'I desire mercy not sacrifice'", that is, not ritual sacrifices, immolations of animals (*Mt* 9:13; *Ho* 6:6).

His whole ministry was a revelation of his mercy to the sick, the possessed, the poor, the unnoticed, the abandoned and, above all, to sinners. The synoptic Gospels characterize Jesus' attitude with a verb derived from the Greek word «σπλαγχνα» (*splagchna*), which meant "bowels or entrails"; the word is not found elsewhere in the Bible with this meaning. It expresses a visceral emotion, namely: that my insides are deeply moved. Do we not say: "my heart is deeply moved?" A leper comes to Jesus and beseeches him, *and his heart was moved*. He had him stretch out his hand, he touched it and said: "I want it, be healed" (*Mk* 1:40). Two blind men heard that Jesus was passing, and they began to cry out: "Lord, have mercy on us!" *Jesus was moved*, he touched their eyes, and healed them (*Mt* 20:34). Seeing the widow of Nain, in the funeral procession of her only son, *the Lord was moved* and he said to her: "Do not weep" and he restored the son to life (*Lk* 7:13). In other passages of the Gospel, Jesus is moved when he sees the crowds: "When he saw the crowds, he had compassion for them, because they were harassed and helpless, like sheep without a shepherd" (*Mt* 9:36). In that case, however, his reaction was different: "And he began to teach them many things", says Mark (*Mk* 6:34). "He healed their sick", says Matthew (*Mt* 14:14). And in one passage, Jesus himself says: "*I have compassion* on the crowd, because they have been with me now three days, and have nothing to eat, and I am unwilling to send them away hungry, lest they faint on the way (*Mt* 15:32). Then he performed the miracle of the loaves. Jesus himself also adopted this word in the parable of the Good Samaritan. The Good Samaritan is *moved* (*Lk* 10:33). Also in the parable of the prodigal son, the father is "*moved*" when he sees the son returning penitent and he runs to him (*Lk* 15:20). Therefore, it is truly characteristic of the attitude of Jesus.

Nevertheless, we cannot conclude that Jesus simply abandons

the struggle against sin. Rather, he leads the struggle in a more radical and efficacious way. Moreover, the battle is against sin, not against sinners and this is precisely the great difference, as we have seen illustrated in the case of the Levites and of Phinehas. Jesus has now taken the fate of sinners upon himself so as to free them from sin. He has borne the struggle in his own person, according to the saving will of the Father. As a consequence or punishment for sin, human death has become for him the means to make love super-abound and to conquer sin and death. He has substituted the total gift of himself for the ancient ritual sacrifices and has obtained what they sought in vain to achieve, namely: perfect communion between man and God.

When the author speaks of Christ's solidarity with us and of his resemblance to his brothers, he excludes sin. Christ is "one who in every respect has been tempted as we are, *yet without sinning*" (*Hb* 4:15). This is of precise importance because, based on the need for a complete solidarity of Christ with us, it could be wrongly deduced that he was also a sinner like us. A protestant exegete has recently supported this completely erroneous deduction. However, the author of the Letter to the Hebrews excludes it categorically, first here and then in another passage, where he states that Christ is our High Priest, "Holy, blameless, unstained" (*Hb* 7:26), who "offered himself without blemish to God" (*Hb* 9:14). In this, the author is in agreement with the whole of the New Testament.

A question could then arise in our hearts: "Does not the absence of all sin in Christ diminish his solidarity with us?" At first sight, it is possible to think that this might be so. However, in reality it is not because sin can never contribute to the establishing of an authentic solidarity. Complicity in sin and solidarity with sinners must never be confused. Sin is always an act of egoism, in one form or another, which creates division and a lack of solidarity; the experience of the scriptures demonstrates this. In Genesis, the persons co-involved begin to accuse one another: the man accuses the woman; the woman accuses the serpent (*Gn* 3:12-13). This is not solidarity. All were accomplices in sin, but no one wished to accept the consequences. The same thing happens in the episode of the golden calf, in Exodus 32: Aaron was the instigator of the people's sin. He said: "Take off the rings of gold which are in the ears of your wives, your sons and your daughters and bring them to me" (*Ex* 32). He melted this gold and fashioned it into a calf. When Moses returned, he interrogated Aaron: "What did this people do to you that you have brought this great sin upon them?" Aaron simply abdicates all responsibility: "Let not the anger of my lord burn hot; you know the people, that they are set on evil. For they said to me, "Make us Gods, who shall go before us" (*Ex* 32:21-23). He accuses the people. Therefore he is not in solidarity with them.

Authentic solidarity with sinners never consists in becoming an accomplice in their sin. This would only aggravate the situation of loss. Rather it consists in generously assuming the dramatic situation caused by sins and in helping sinners to leave that place of sin. Such is the generosity of God. He has taken upon himself our sins and even the sins of all sinful men. Furthermore, he has taken upon himself the punishment of the worst criminals, namely: the cross. God has done this, although he has contributed nothing to the guilt of mankind, nothing at all to deserve punishment. As a result, every person, even the most sinful and most guilty, when he suffers on account of his own sins, can feel the presence of Jesus at his side. Even the worst criminals find themselves hanging condemned beside the cross of Jesus who is merciful and compassionate and will soon open paradise to them. Luke demonstrates this in recounting the story of the good thief (*Lk* 23:39-43).

Also, with regard to sin, we can note a contrast with the Old Testament. The Old Testament was very preoccupied with the purity of priests, since it was rightly recognized as an indispensable condition for entering into relationship with God. Therefore, absolute purity was required of the priest. However, this was merely a ritual purity. It was not in any way a requirement of sacerdotal sinlessness. This could not have been required because no one was without sin. On the contrary, when the Book of Leviticus deals with the sacrifices for sin, the first case considered is the sin of the High Priest himself (*Lv* 4:3). Likewise on Kippur, the day of the great expiation, the first expiatory sacrifice is that of the High Priest (*Lv* 6:12).

In the New Testament, the situation is completely turned around. While in the Old Testament, we find a High Priest who is a sinner, namely, Aaron, who is devoid of compassion for sinners, in the New Testament we welcome a High Priest who is without sin and is full of compassion for sinners. We find ourselves faced with the most profound revelation of the generous love and gratuity of God and it is a truly amazing revelation.

So, it follows that we can now approach the throne of God with confidence as the author affirms: "Let us then with confidence draw near to the throne of grace, that we may receive mercy and find grace to help in time of need" (*Hb* 4:16). In the Old Testament, God's throne was a seat of frightening holiness. It is enough to recall Isaiah's trepidation when he had a vision in the Temple: "Woe is me! For I am lost; for I am a man of unclean lips" (*Is* 6:5). This throne, thanks to Christ, has become "the throne of grace". It is the throne of gratuitous, generous and merciful love because Christ is seated beside God and he is our compassionate brother who intercedes for us. Therefore, we are invited to draw near to this throne with full confidence, that is, with the certainty of receiving mercy, of finding grace and of being helped in time of need. This is our situation in the New Covenant. It is a situation that is full of hope and we are called to enter it. We need to receive the boundless mercy of Christ in the sacrament of reconciliation. It is a situation into which we are also called to lead others on account of our trustworthiness. We have the task of propagating the good news: we have a High

Priest who is capable of sharing our weakness and who desires to help and save us.

7
The Priestly Solidarity of Christ
(Hb 5:1-10)

After having presented Christ our merciful High Priest to us, the author of the Letter to the Hebrews leads us to meditate, at the beginning of chapter 5, on the nature of the priesthood and its fulfillment in Christ. The first four verses of this chapter are seemingly a general description of the priesthood but in reality they point quite specifically to priestly solidarity with sinners. Starting from verse 5, the author goes on to apply this description to Christ within the same perspective.

The description of the priesthood comprises three successive elements: the first is a general definition which affirms the priest's twofold relationship with men and with God (5:1); the second is a more precise determination of his relationship with sinful men (5:2-3); the third is a specific explanation of his relationship with God (5:4).

The definition (*Hb* 5:1) reads: "For every High Priest chosen from among men is appointed to act on behalf of men in relation to God". This definition clearly shows that the priest is a mediator between men and God, and it especially insists on the solidarity between the priest and the people. It is a definition that is characteristic of the author's doctrine and the perspective of the New Testament. The Old Testament was unilaterally concerned for the priest's relationship with God. In Exodus 28:1, God says to Moses: "Then bring near to you Aaron, your brother, and his sons with him, from among the people of Israel, to *serve me* as priests". Similarly, in Exodus 30:30: "And you shall anoint Aaron and his sons, and consecrate them, that they may *serve me* as priests (*li* in Hebrew, *moi* in Greek)". The priest is a man of worship who stands at God's service. Instead, the author of the Letter has the audacity to say: "For every High Priest chosen from among men is appointed to act on behalf of men in relation to God". He insists on a twofold bond of solidarity that ties the priest to men. It is a bond according to origin, for the priest has been taken from among men. Furthermore, it is a bond of finality, for he is appointed to act on their behalf in relation to God. Then, on the other side of the mediation is expressed, of course, the relationship with God: the High Priest has been appointed to act in relation to God.

The author immediately specifies that this priestly mediation is exercised in the offering of gifts and sacrifices for sins. In priestly mediation, there are in reality, three successive steps: firstly, there is a movement of ascent to God through the offering of sacrifices; then there is the encounter with God; finally there is a descent so as to bring God's gifts to the people. The author speaks here only of the movement of ascent, namely, the offering of sacrifices so as to overcome the obstacle that separates the people from God. Effectively, this movement is decisive for all the rest. It also manifests the priest's solidarity with man. In the verses which follow, the author will insist on this solidarity, explaining that the High Priest "...can deal gently with the ignorant and the wayward" – literally, "Have moderate feelings for" – "since he himself is beset with weakness" (Heb 5:2).

Ignorance and error tend to lessen guilt. The Old Testament clearly distinguished between two categories of sins: sins into which one falls through ignorance or through inadvertence (*Nb* 15:22-29); those approved and applauded with "a show of hands", that is, transgressions committed with full knowledge and open rebellion (*Nb* 15:30-31). For this second category of sin, no sacrificial expiation was foreseen. He who openly rebelled against

God must be "eliminated" (*Nb* 15:30-31). For the first category, however, there could be and must be a sacrificial expiation.

In the New Testament, there is a tendency to put all sins in the category of ignorance, believing that deep down, the sinner is never aware of the gravity of his sin, as Jesus' own words in response to the most horrendous sin of the crucifixion lead us to understand: "Father, forgive them; for they know not what they do" (*Lk* 23:34). Peter says to the Jews in one of his first discourses: "And now, brethren, I know that you acted in ignorance as did also your rulers" (*Acts* 3:17). Peter lessens the culpability not only of the people but also even of their leaders, that is, of the Sanhedrin.

Therefore, the High Priest is able to deal gently with the ignorant and the wayward, that is, with sinful men because he too has shared their condition of weakness, which in the Old Testament included sin. Here, the author is referring to the passages of the Old Testament that prescribe that the High Priest offer sacrifices, first for his own sins, and then for those of the people.

After pointing out, in this way, the aspect of solidarity between the High Priest and the people, the author makes a further determination concerning relationships with God. This is the third element of the description. "And one does not take the honour upon himself, but he is called by God, just as Aaron was" (*Hb* 5:4). The priesthood cannot be a human conquest; it is a gift that completely depends on God's initiative and therefore must continue to be received with humility. Effectively, the first High Priest, Aaron, did not name himself, but was chosen and nominated by God. An episode of the Book of Numbers, which I have already highlighted, strongly suggests this condition on the basis of which one would not take for himself the priesthood in order to put himself over others, but would only receive it humbly from God if he conferred it so as to be placed at the service of others for dealings with God. I am referring to the episode of Korah and his two accomplices who wished to take the priesthood for themselves. God's response was clear and tremendous. The ambitious were exterminated (*Nb* 16:31-35). In this whole description, the author has remained faithful to the perspective of the solidarity of the priest with other men.

In verse 5, he then goes on to consider the case of Christ. This description also contains three successive elements, which correspond to the three elements in the preceding description, except in the opposite order, as often happens in the Bible. The first affirmation concerns Christ's humility, that is, his renunciation of self-glorification. The author literally writes: "So also Christ did not exult himself to be made a High Priest". The translations are often a little inexact. Christ did not glorify himself. His priesthood was not the fruit of ambition. It was not attained by a self-glorification. On the contrary it was obtained by means of a voluntary humiliation, as will be explained immediately after. Christ was proclaimed Priest by God following his priestly consecration that consisted in the most complete solidarity with men to the point of death. This is the great newness of his priesthood. The author then describes the way in which Christ has become High Priest. Christ has become High Priest through his Passion and has then been proclaimed Priest by God according to the oracle of Psalm 109/110: "You are priest". The author cites it here. "He who said to him: 'Thou art my son, today I have begotten thee'; as he says also in another place, 'Thou art a priest forever, after the order of Melchizedek'." Certainly, Christ was already destined for this priesthood from the first moment. However, the moment at which he attained it was His Passion: "In the days of his flesh, Jesus offered up prayers and supplications, with loud cries and tears, to him who was able to save him from death, and he was heard for his godly fear. Although he was a Son, he learned obedience through what he suffered; and being made perfect he became the source of eternal salvation to all who obey him, being designated by God a high priest after the order of Melchizedek"

(*Hb* 5:7-10). This is a very dense passage. It is a passage full of doctrine. It is a true revelation.

In these verses, a dramatic oblation has been evoked. The tone is very different from that of the preceding phrases, which were didactic and in the style of a definition. Now it becomes dramatic. The expression "In the days of his flesh" point to the weakness of the man who is exposed to suffering and death. Jesus' Passion is presented as an oblation, a sacrifice and, at the same time, a plea. The author demonstrates that Christ has indeed made himself one with us sinners. In Gethsemane, he experiences a dramatic anguish that leads him to prayer and to beseech him who is able to save him from death. It leads him not only to pray and to entreat but also to cry out and to weep. The author is referring, evidently and firstly, to Jesus' agony in Gethsemane. However, he is also referring to the cry of Jesus on the cross. He also adds to that the tears, which are not mentioned in the Gospel accounts of the passion but in other episodes (cf. *Lk* 19:41; *Jn* 11:35).

Jesus' Passion is presented both as a supplication and as an oblation. However, this seems to be paradoxical. In themselves, oblation and supplication are entirely distinct. However, the author immediately says that Jesus "offered supplication". The Greek word here is really «προσφερειν», "to offer", which is sometimes weakened in translation, because the expression is strange. However, in an authentic prayer, we must understand that these attitudes must always go together. When we ask for grace, we must also offer our availability to God. We cannot impose our way of seeing things on God. To demand or to require that he intervene according to our directions would be to impose on him. We must allow God the freedom to choose the solution. This is what Jesus did. On the other hand, when we offer something to God, we must ask God that he sanctify our offering, that he adapt it according to his grace and transform it. Otherwise, our offering will be deprived of value. Therefore, our offerings should be made with an attitude of supplication and our supplications with an attitude of oblation. In his agony, Jesus prayed: he asked, "My Father, if it be possible, let this cup pass from me" (*Mt* 26:29). But he immediately expressed an attitude of offering: "Nevertheless, not as I will, but as thou wilt" (*Mt* 36:29). He has offered to do the will of the Father. In this, his request has attained an aspect of oblation.

Jesus has been heard, says the author, and has effectively been saved from death but in the way chosen by the Father. There are three possible ways of being saved from death. The first consists in being preserved from death and receiving an extension of life. For example, when King Hezekiah was suffering from a terminal illness, he besought God and obtained another fifteen years of life (*2K* 20:6). It is a solution that is positive but provisional. After 15 years, Hezekiah would still have to die. The second solution is to die and to be restored to earthly life, like Lazarus (*Jn* 11:43-44): this is a miraculous solution, but also one that is provisional. The third solution is to die in such a way as to obtain, through death, the definitive and complete victory over death itself. This would be the perfect solution. It is indeed the solution that Christ obtained. By means of death, he conquered death by offering himself as the supreme gift of love. For this reason, the author can say that Christ, having offered prayer and supplication, was heard for his Godly fear.

The author continues: "Although he was a Son, he learned obedience through what he suffered". In these words, it seems to me that the most profound mystery of redemption is expressed. The assertion that Jesus learned obedience in his Passion is certainly surprising, but this does not imply that Jesus had been disobedient prior to the Passion. The author of the Letter to the Hebrews, in chapter 10, emphasizes that upon entering into the world, indeed from the first moment, Christ says: "Lo, I have come to do thy will, O God" (*Hb* 10:5-9). Therefore, Jesus had, from the beginning, a perfect and prior disposition to obedience.

However, it is necessary to make an important distinction between the prior disposition to obedience and the virtue attained by obedience and acquired through temptation. For our human nature, the two things are indeed entirely distinct. Only he who faces and overcomes the hardest temptations acquires the virtue of obedience in every fibre of his human nature. At the beginning, he may have been disposed to obedience, but this was not yet the acquired virtue. It is a law of our human nature and Jesus accepted that law. The Incarnation involves this aspect. In himself, he did not need this suffering education. The author says that, although he was Son, he needed to learn through his human nature, just like we do. On the other hand, his obedience was superabundant in the sense that, through his solidarity with us, Christ accepted a fate that he had not at all merited. So his obedience overflows to us. Christ is able to communicate to us his profound docility to God.

Here, we can catch on better, it seems to me, to the meaning of the Incarnation and redemption. Jesus has assumed our human nature in its fallen state. He has assumed, says St Paul in his Letter to the Philippians, "the form of a servant" («δουλος») (*Phil* 2:7), not the condition of a son. Furthermore, he was sent "in the likeness of sinful flesh", according to his Letter to the Romans (*Rm* 8:3). Christ has assumed this nature of ours in order to transform it and to conform it more perfectly to God's plan. This is the true meaning of redemption. With an amazing generosity, Christ has accepted being subjected to our place, in our favour, to the suffering education that was indispensable for us. Therefore, "being made perfect, he became the source of eternal salvation to all who obey him, being designated by God a High Priest after the order of Melchizedek" (*Hb* 5:9-10). This is the author's triumphant conclusion.

He has been "made perfect". This statement is also very surprising, because we spontaneously think that Christ was perfect from the beginning; he did not need to be made perfect.

But this thinking does not correspond to an adequate concept of the Incarnation according to which, "becoming man" is a way toward perfection. St Luke tells us explicitly that the Christ child "increased" (*RSV*) not only "in age" but also "in wisdom and in stature, and in favour with God and man" (*Lk* 2:52). Jesus, as a child, did not have the perfection of an adult; he had to acquire it through various hardships. Jesus, as an adult, did not yet have the perfection of the priesthood. He had to acquire it through his Passion. He had, in other words, to bring the two relationships that are indispensable for the exercise of priestly mediation to their full perfection, namely: the relationship with God and the relationship with his brothers.

These two relationships were subjected to extreme tension when Jesus experienced himself to be abandoned by God and given as prey to the wickedness of men. However, they have resisted the tension and been reciprocally reinforced. Christ has brought them to perfection through his sufferings and his death, which he accepted in filial obedience and in fraternal solidarity. His relationship to the Father has acquired the highest level of perfection thanks to his filial obedience that endured, even to death on the cross. His relationship to us has therefore acquired the highest level of perfection thanks to his fraternal solidarity that also endured until death, as a result of condemnation. Christ has, therefore, in this way, been made perfect and has been *consecrated priest.*

Indeed, the Greek word adopted by the author («τελεωθεις» - «*teleioun*») has these two meanings. In itself, it means, "to make perfect", but in the Greek translation of the Pentateuch, it was adopted exclusively to mean: to consecrate priest (Cf. *Ex* 29:9, 29, 33, 35, etc). Furthermore, in chapter 7, the author has highlighted this use of the Pentateuch (Cf. *Hb* 7:11, 19, 28). So, the verb, in religious language, has the connotation of priestly consecrating. The perfection acquired by Jesus in his passion was effectively a priestly perfection, a perfection that came from being a mediator between men and God. It is a perfection that the High Priests of the Old Testament were never able to achieve.

This text is very profound. It merits a lengthy meditation. It helps us to understand the priestly consecration of Christ, his priesthood itself and our participation in this priesthood. The sacrament of Orders, which we have received, takes its whole value and its entire efficacy from the fact that it has placed us in a relationship of intimacy with Christ's priestly consecration. All the sacraments find their value in relation to the Passion. However, this is especially so for the sacrament of Orders. This sacrament has communicated to us the twofold dynamism that is characteristic of Christ's consecration, namely: the dynamic of filial obedience to God; and the dynamic of a fraternal solidarity with men. Let us always consider these two attitudes well because their union is essential for priestly mediation and for pastoral ministry; let us ask the Lord to give us this fundamental grace. Thanks to the Passion of Jesus, we can better understand our ministerial priesthood.

8
The Promise of a New Covenant
(Jer 31:31-34)

The Letter to the Hebrews establishes an intimate and original connection between priesthood and covenant. This connection is not noticed in the Old Testament. However, between Christ's Priesthood and the New Covenant, the relationship is very close. Christ is called "the mediator of a New Covenant" and in this sense he is High Priest. In preparation for this statement (*Hb* 9:15), the author quotes integrally the oracle of Jeremiah who announced the New Covenant (*Jr* 31:31-34; *Hb* 8:8-12). It is the longest citation of the Old Testament in the New.

I propose to you to meditate on this oracle. It is one of the most beautiful passages in the Old Testament. In the Old Testament, beautiful promises were often mixed with promises of material prosperity: an abundance of fruit or cattle and such things. In the oracle of the New Covenant, the promise that is given is an intimate relationship with God:

> Behold, the days are coming, says the Lord, when I will make a New Covenant with the house of Israel and the house of Judah, not like the covenant which I made with their fathers when I took them by the hand to bring them out of the land of Egypt, my covenant which they broke, though I was their husband, says the Lord. But this is the covenant which I will make with the house of Israel after those days, says the Lord: "I will put my law within them, and I will write it upon their hearts; and I will be their God,

and they shall be my people. And no longer shall each man teach his neighbour and each his brother, saying, 'Know the Lord', for they shall all know me, from the least of them to the greatest, says the Lord; for I will forgive their iniquity, and I will remember their sin no more (*Jr* 31:31-34).

This is a splendid promise; an amazing initiative of God. It is not about a covenant that would be the fruit of bilateral discussions aimed at a mutual agreement and a promise of reciprocal help. Rather, it is about a divine initiative that is gratuitous and generous. "I will make a New Covenant". Why this initiative of God? The oracle explains it. The Israelites have not remained faithful to the covenant agreed upon at the time of the Exodus; therefore, a new initiative was necessary.

At the time of the Exodus, God had freed his people from slavery in Egypt. He had saved them from extermination and led them into the desert so as to make a covenant with them. God's plan was a beautiful plan of love. We see it in chapter 19 of Exodus: "Now, therefore, if you will obey my voice and keep my covenant, you shall be my own possession among all peoples; for all the earth is mine, and you shall be to me a kingdom of priests and a holy nation" (*Ex* 19:5-6). The Covenant had stipulated a promise of fidelity that was signed with the blood of animals so as to symbolize the living union between God and his people (*Ex* 24:4-8). However, this agreement was broken by the people only a short time later. We see this in the episode of the Golden Calf, which is the first narrative episode following the covenant agreement. (*Ex* 32). The chapters in between are legislative rather than narrative.

This situation was continually repeated in the history of the people of Israel. In particular, the time in which Jeremiah lived was a time of constant infidelity and breaking of the Covenant (cf. *2 Ch* 36:15-16). Then the terrible catastrophe occurs: the Chaldean army marches against Jerusalem, besieges the city, captures it, burns the Temple and the inhabitants are carried off into exile (*2 K* 25). It is the terrible outcome of the breaking of the Covenant. It is precisely in this situation that God commands the prophet to announce his completely new and gratuitous initiative, the promise of the New Covenant. It is not just a matter of a renewed covenant. This one is indeed new. However, there had been occasions of covenant renewal: the first took place immediately after the episode of the Golden Calf, as the Book of Exodus tells us: "The LORD said to Moses, "Cut two tables of stone like the first; and I will write upon the tables the words that were on the first tables, which you broke" (*Ex* 34:1). There is no new covenant here; the tablets must be the same as the first; they must be tablets of stone like the first; they must be cut in the same way as the first; the same words must be written on them. However, Jeremiah's oracle states: "I will make a new covenant with the house of Israel and the house of Judah, not like the covenant which I made with their fathers". While the text of Exodus insists on the sameness, the text of Jeremiah clearly insists on the difference. This can easily be understood following the repeated breaking of the first Covenant. God does not wish to re-establish something that has shown itself to be less than adequate, even inefficacious. In any case, it would most likely fail again. God wants to make a radical change. This is what he promises in the oracle of Jeremiah. So, the author of the Letter to the Hebrews states: "In speaking of a New Covenant, he treats the first as obsolete. And what is becoming obsolete and growing old is ready to vanish away" (*Hb* 8:13). In what does the newness of this Covenant consist? To be precise, it consists in four aspects: the first aspect is that the New Covenant will be interior, not exterior; the second aspect is that it will be a relationship of perfect reciprocity between God and his people; the third aspect is that it will not be a collective institution but will involve the personal relationship of each individual with God; the fourth aspect is that this relationship will be founded upon the complete forgiveness of sins. This final aspect manifests the full divine immensity that forms the basis of the New Covenant.

The first aspect is the transformation of the heart. The New Covenant will be an interior Covenant: "I will put my laws into their minds, and write them on their hearts". This is in clear contrast to the old law. On Sinai, God had written his laws onto two tablets of stone. It was external, a code of laws to be observed. It did nothing at all to change the heart of the person. We are told that the people had a wicked heart that was always being led astray. This is affirmed in an array of Old Testament texts. God would lament: "This people draw near with their mouth and honour me with their lips while their hearts are far from me" (*Is* 29:13) "They are a people that err in heart, and they do not regard my ways" (*Ps* 94/95:10).

If the heart is wicked, of what use are laws? Ultimately, even the best laws are of no use if there is still a desire to transgress the law. In his letter to the Romans, St Paul helps us to understand this well: "If it had not been for the law, I should not have known sin. I should not have known what it is to covet if the law had not said, 'You shall not covet'. But sin, finding opportunity in the commandment, wrought in me all kinds of covetousness" (*Rm* 7:7-8). St Paul also says that the law was given so that sin might abound (*Rm* 5:20). An interior transformation was also necessary and this is precisely what God promised. To have God's laws written on one's own heart meant having a docile heart that would be capable of freely fulfilling God's will, out of love. It meant being convinced that God's law is the best thing for the person. This is the requirement and at the same time the promise that God makes: "I will put my law within them, and I will write it upon their hearts" (*Jr* 31:33). Once the heart has been changed, a perfect reciprocal relationship between God and his people is established: "I will be their God, and they shall be my people". Here we have the typical formula of the Covenant. It is repeated many times in the Old Testament, but always with the future verb, as something still to be achieved. However, there was a prior condition that had never been properly fulfilled: "Listen to my voice, and do all that I command you. So shall you be my people, and I will be your God" (Jr 11:4). The prophets would always have to challenge the people's infidelity, which obstructed this plan of reciprocity. Instead, when the law of God is written on the heart, perfect reciprocity is secured.

Allowing himself to be guided by inspiration, Jeremiah has the audacity to announce that instead of being a collective institution, like the Covenant of Sinai, the New Covenant will consist in a personal relationship of each person with God. It will be an intimate relationship that will render admonitions useless. "No longer shall each man teach his neighbour and teach his brother saying, 'Know the Lord', for they shall all know me, from the least of the them to the greatest, says the Lord" (Jr 31:34). In the Old Testament, we see that prophetic warnings and threats were always needed. However, they will no longer be needed in the New Covenant because each person will know the Lord. In biblical language, to know a person means to have a personal relationship with him or her. In our present context, it does not refer to an intellectual acknowledgement of God's existence but to being united with him through a profound personal relationship.

The situation announced by Jeremiah constitutes a complete change. Certainly, the prophets often had to complain with disappointment that the people did not know the Lord, that they did not have a true relationship with him. Isaiah writes: "The ox knows its owner and the ass its master's crib; but Israel does not know, my people do not understand" (Is 1:3). Furthermore, we find in Jeremiah, "For they proceed from evil to evil, and they do not know me" (Jr 1:3). Therefore, the prophets received from the Lord the mission of reproving the Israelites and of crying out to them that they might listen: "Go and proclaim in the hearing of Jerusalem" (Jr 2:2); "Cry aloud, spare not, lift up your voice like a trumpet; declare to my people their transgression, to the house of Jacob their sins" (Is 58:1). The prophet's intervention would fail to bring about a conversion. God had already predicted this to Jeremiah, saying: "You shall speak all these words to them, but they will not listen to you. You shall call to them, but they will not answer you" (Jr 7:27). The oracle of the New Covenant announces a diametrically different situation. It will no longer be necessary to instruct one's own brother since all will have their own personal relationship to God: "For they shall all know me, from the least of them to the greatest" (Jr 31:34). This is a marvellous ideal and it corresponds to other promises made by God through the lips of the prophets as we see for example in this quote from Isaiah: "All your sons shall be taught by the Lord" (Is 54:13). "For the earth shall be full of the knowledge of the Lord as the waters cover the sea" (Is 11:9).

Significantly, each of the above three aspects is based on the fourth and final aspect of the oracle, namely: the forgiveness of sins: "For I will forgive their iniquity; and I will remember their sin no more" (Jr 31:34). This is stupendous forgiveness. It reveals to us the boundless generosity of God whose paternal love is full of mercy. At the time of Jeremiah, forgiveness seemed impossible due to the people's obstinacy as much as to their continued rebellion and infidelity. God noted the misdeeds of his people and asked Jeremiah if forgiveness might be possible. At one stage, God even forbids the prophet to intercede for the people: "As for you, do not pray for this people, or lift up cry or pray for them, and do not intercede with me, for I do not hear you" (Jr 7:16). We find ourselves facing a situation of complete infidelity on the part of the people. Forgiveness seemed impossible. But God thinks of them again in his boundless generosity and promises to offer a total forgiveness that will enable each person to have a new and intimate relationship with him.

The oracle of Jeremiah therefore opens marvellous perspectives, but it does not explain how this extraordinary promise of God can be achieved. This would only be revealed by Jesus at the Last Supper, at the Institution of the Eucharist. Jesus took the chalice and said, "This is my blood of the Covenant" (*Mt* 26:28; *Mk* 14:24). The New Covenant must be established in blood, like the first Covenant; not in the blood of animals, but in the blood of Jesus, a blood "which is poured out for many for the forgiveness of sins" (*Mt* 26:28), according to the promise of the New Covenant: "I will forgive their iniquity (*Jr* 31:34).

Let us meditate on this marvellous promise in the light of the Eucharist. Let us ask for the grace to truly receive this divine promise and to perceive all its extraordinary newness. We did not merit the New Covenant; we do not have anything deserving of merit. It is a gratuitous, generous and merciful initiative of God. We live in the time of this New Covenant, but we must take heed of its novelty, which renews us completely and establishes us in a profound and intimate relationship with God through Christ, the mediator of the New Covenant.

9
The Wedding Feast of Cana:
Sign of a New Covenant (Jn 2:1-11)

In order to deepen the theme of Christ as the Mediator of the New Covenant, I propose to you that we temporarily leave the Letter to the Hebrews at this point and take into consideration a Gospel episode, in which Jesus, in a rather profound and implicit way, manifests himself as the Mediator of a New Covenant. I have in mind the episode of the wedding feast of Cana. It is a significant moment. There was a wedding at Cana in Galilee and it was celebrated in order to establish a covenant, that is: a nuptial covenant. Jesus' mother was there too. During the celebration, Jesus, at the request of his mother, transformed water into choice, abundant wine and enabled the wedding feast to continue according to plans. The evangelist underlines the great importance of this episode when he affirms at the end: "This, the first of his signs, Jesus did at Cana in Galilee, and he manifested his glory; and his disciples believed in him" (*Jn* 2:11).

The translations often say: "Jesus worked the first of his miracles", but John uses the Greek term *«σημεῖον»*, which means sign, because the evangelist wants us to turn our attention to the meaning of the event, rather than lingering, as we spontaneously tend to do, on the prodigious and sensational aspects. So, in the fourth Gospel, the accounts of the "signs" are often followed by long doctrinal explanations. However, the "sign" of the wedding feast of Cana is not immediately followed by a commentary. Nevertheless, in the following chapter, an explanation is suggested when the evangelist refers to a discussion that arises between the disciples of the Baptist and a Jew regarding purification (*Jn* 3:25). In the "sign" of Cana, the six stone water jars were there "for the Jewish rites of purification" (*Jn* 2:6). At the request of his disciples, John the Baptist responds: "I am not the Christ, but I have been sent before him. He who has the bride is the bridegroom; the friend of the bridegroom, who stands and hears him, rejoices greatly at the bridegroom's voice; therefore, this joy of mine is now full" (*Jn* 3:28-29). The joy of the Baptist is that of hearing the voice of the spouse. The spouse is Jesus. On the other hand, Jesus' discourse following the multiplication of the loaves also helps us to comment on the episode at Cana because he not only speaks of food but also of drink.

In order to understand in depth the episode of the wedding feast of Cana, we must refer to the Old Testament, where the theme of the wedding feast of God with the chosen race is continually present. It is a metaphorical way to speak of the covenant. In pure love, God has chosen a spouse, namely: Israel, who is also called the "daughter of Sion". Israel is represented in the feminine. To her, the Lord has proposed in a nuptial covenant. God wants to be the husband of Israel but the condition is that the people reciprocate this divine desire and be faithful to the Covenant. Unfortunately, this condition was never properly met. The marriage began but it could not be brought to fulfillment. Despite the generosity of God, the people showed themselves to be unfaithful time and again. As you know, in the Old Testament, idolatry was likened to an unfaithful marriage, to adultery and even to prostitution. The Book of Exodus relates the episode of the Golden Calf (*Ex* 32), which was the first occasion of Israel's prostitution. It follows closely upon the agreement of the Covenant of Sinai. The Covenant is hardly concluded and we have the first historical account of the people's idolatry.

The prophet Ezekiel, in chapter 16 of his book narrates a history of love and infidelity; it is God himself who relates the story to Ezekiel in much detail. Other prophets, in less realistic or detailed language than Ezekiel, relate the situation of Israel's adultery and the impossibility of her establishing relations with God. Through the lips of Hosea, the Lord openly declares to the Israelites: "Plead with your mother, plead – for she is not my wife, and I am not her husband – that she put away her harlotry from her face, and her adultery from between her breasts" (*Ho* 2:2). She has broken faith. Many prophets threatened punishments, describing the punishments that God will inflict on his own people. The imagery that they use is important, for it involves the privation of weddings and the absence of joy. From the moment that the people were unfaithful to God, they were no longer allowed to celebrate even human marriage feasts, at least, not according to the prophets. Jeremiah in particular, after recalling the many violations of the Covenant in chapter 7, relates the Lord's conclusion: "And I will make to cease from the cities of Judah and from the streets of Jerusalem, the voice of mirth, the voice of the bridegroom and the voice of the bride; for the land shall become a waste." (*Jr* 7:34). The prophet also receives orders not to participate in any marriage ceremonies or banquets. Other prophets announced the privation of wine. For example: "The wine mourns, the vine languishes, all the merry-hearted sigh... No more do they drink wine with singing" (*Is* 24:7,9). There will be no more marriage feasts and no more wine because the people have transgressed the law, they have disobeyed the Lord and they have broken the covenant of love (*Is* 24:5).

But even in the most tragic moments, the Lord does not renounce his plan of union in love. He still wants to bring the marriage with his people to fulfillment. So he promises a New Covenant and the joys of the marriage feast where the abundance of wine will again be possible. In Jeremiah, in chapter 33, after the announcement of the New Covenant, the Lord promises: "Thus says the Lord: in this place of which you say, 'it is a waste without man or beast', in the cities of Judah and the streets of Jerusalem that are desolate, without man or inhabitant or beast, there shall never be heard again the voice of mirth and the voice of gladness, the voice of the bridegroom and the voice of the bride" (*Jr* 33:10-11). Through the lips of Ezekiel, God promises: "Yet I will remember my covenant with you in the days of your youth, and I will establish with you an everlasting covenant (*Ez* 16:60). God, therefore, manifests an extraordinary constancy and an amazing generosity: he always re-proposes the Covenant to his people.

The episode of the wedding feast of Cana should be read in this context: the wedding celebrations had already begun, as they had begun for the Israelites at the time of the Exodus. However, the problem at Cana was the lack of wine. Without it, the nuptial celebrations could not be brought to fulfillment. At this point, Mary presented the situation to Jesus and Jesus intervened. Firstly, he ordered the stone water jars to be filled: the evangelist observes here that water served the requirement for ritual purification among the Jews. That is what the six stone water jars were there for (*Jn* 2:6). The water in the stone jars corresponded exactly to the situation of the Old Covenant: a system of external purification that was incapable of establishing an interior covenant because the law was written on stone and not on hearts. This water would not enable the nuptial celebrations to attain their fulfillment. So a radical change was necessary. Jesus worked this change: after the water had been placed in the jars, he offered it as a new wine, an excellent wine, to the master of the table. Everyone marveled at its quality.

The disciples were able to recognize Jesus' glory in what he had done. His glory is the glory of the promised Messiah who is capable of restoring the abundance of wine and of making the fulfillment of the nuptial celebration possible. Jesus' glory is the glory of the bridegroom, because in this episode, the true bridegroom is not the one celebrating his own wedding who in no way was able to procure the much needed wine: the true bridegroom is Jesus. Jesus' glory is the glory of the generous love that gives the good wine and brings the nuptial celebrations to their fulfillment.

But what is the meaning of the wine? The wine of Cana is a sign. It is the sign of another very important reality. At this point of the Gospel, we do not know the meaning of the wine. Neither did the disciples; it would become known later on. In chapter 6 of John's Gospel, after the multiplication of the loaves, the theme of drink is introduced. The Lord says: "He who eats my flesh and drinks my blood abides in me, and I in him" (*Jn.*6:56). The good wine, of which the wine of Cana was only a sign, is the blood of Jesus. It is the generous gift that Christ makes of his life so as to make the fulfillment of the nuptial feast possible. There cannot be a more intimate covenant for us than this communion. It is a reciprocal interiority that the Lord offers, saying: "He who eats my flesh and drinks my blood abides in me, and I in him". It is the perfect covenant. Therefore, the discourse of the bread of life anticipates the Last Supper when Jesus would take the cup and say: "This is my blood of the Covenant, which is poured out for many" (*Mk* 14:24). Later on, on Calvary, the good wine will flow out from the heart of Christ and that will be the precise moment of the fulfillment of the wedding feast (*Jn* 19:34). The episode of Cana was only a sign, but it was a very important sign. This aspect of the wedding feast does not appear on Calvary but, thanks to Cana, we know that it concerns the fulfillment of the Messianic nuptial feast.

In this perspective, we also need to see the figure of Mary. The evangelist notes that Mary was at Cana before Jesus. "On the third day, there was a marriage at Cana in Galilee, and the mother of Jesus was there" (*Jn* 2:1). So it seems that Jesus had been invited to this marriage on account of the presence of his mother. Noticing that the wine had run out, Mary turns to Jesus and says to him: "They have no wine" (*Jn* 2:3). With the heart of a mother, she is attentive to the needs of people and she puts the case to Jesus as a mother speaks to her own son.

However, something unexpected happens with Jesus' reaction to his mother's words, "They have no wine". Her words don't even sound like a request. Mary has not asked him anything. Jesus says: "Oh woman, what have you to do with me?" (*RSV* translation) We are faced with a disconcerting reaction. The Greek text literally says: "What to me and to you?" The expression is found quite frequently in the Old Testament. It always indicates that a relationship between persons is being questioned. It can equally be used to question either a hostile or an amicable relationship. For example, when David had to flee Jerusalem on account of Absalom's rebellion, he used this formula with regard to one of his officials, so as to prevent him killing one of Saul's household who was insulting David (*2 Sam* 16:10). There is also the case of the widow who offered hospitality to Elijah: the son of this widow was ill and dying. When the prophet arrives, the widow consults him and asks him about her relationship with him: "What have you against me, oh man of God" (*RSV*), (*1 K* 17:18). So the expression always implies that a relationship is being questioned.

With this expression, Jesus now wants to question his familial relationship to his mother and to suggest that this relationship must now give way to new kind of relationship. Indeed, to indicate this change, instead of saying "Mother", Jesus uses the word, "Woman": "What to me and to you, 'Woman'?" This way of relating to a woman in public was not rude; it was normal. Jesus also uses this expression for the Canaanite woman, for the Samaritan woman and for Mary Magdalene. But it does not seem normal on the lips of a son who is speaking to his own mother. Nevertheless, by using this expression, Jesus makes it known that he does not intend to place himself on a familial level. This attitude of Jesus corresponds to one that we find in other episodes referred to in the Synoptics. For example, on one such occasion, when Jesus was speaking to his followers, his brothers (relatives) and his mother came looking for him. Jesus again questioned his familial relationships: "Who is my mother? Who are my brothers?" Pointing to the disciples, he said, "Here are my mother and my brethren! For whoever does the will of my Father in heaven is my brother, and sister, and mother" (*Mt* 12:48-50). Mary must, therefore, accept the development of her relationship with her son. Actually, this is a normal aspect of family life. Between a mother and a son, there is always need for change and development in their reciprocal relationship which is never easy. It presupposes, on the part of the mother, the capacity to accept that the son is progressively distancing himself from her, assuming his own autonomy. At the beginning, the baby is in his mother's womb, then he is in her arms, then he walks, then finally he leaves her.

Jesus uses another expression that is usually translated as a negative declaration: "My hour has not yet come". However, we must keep in mind that in the oldest manuscripts, punctuation marks were not used. There is nothing to indicate to us whether or not this phrase is negative or interrogative. Most interpret it as a negative declaration. However, good exegetes have from patristic times interpreted it as interrogative and still do to our day. Jesus asks: "Surely my hour has not yet arrived?" It must be said that this interpretation seems to me to be the right interpretation. For one reason that is a little unique, namely, that a question allows the possibility of various responses. A negative declaration, instead, closes the discourse. The question of Jesus suggests at first sight, a positive response: the hour of Jesus is near. A patristic commentary explains that now it is no longer the hour of Mary, that is, the time in which the mother had to guide her son's life; it is now the hour of Jesus, the hour in which Jesus must take the initiative and achieve on God's level. Jesus does not have to obey Mary any more. He must take in hand his own mission of Messiah, demonstrate his authority, and manifest his glory. This is the will of the Father. A question, however, always allows the possibility of various responses, and does not suggest any. Jesus' question, therefore, allows the possibility of adding a negative response at another level and this seems to me to correspond to the intention of the evangelist who most often poses these questions which require a two-fold response: one that is positive in a certain perspective and another that is negative at another level. For example, at a certain moment, Jesus says to the Jews: "I go away, and you will seek me and die in your sin; where I am going, you cannot come" (*Jn* 8:21-22). The response is negative, Jesus will not kill himself; he will be killed through the intervention of his enemies. But in the fourth Gospel, the response can also be positive; indeed, it must be positive because Jesus said of his life: "No one takes it from me, but I lay it down of my own accord" (*Jn* 10:18). In another passage, the Jews ask if Jesus will go to evangelize the Greeks (*Jn* 7:35). Certainly, during his own earthly life, Jesus would not go to evangelize the Greeks; afterwards, however, through his Paschal Mystery, he will effectively go and evangelize the Greeks and other peoples (Cf. *Jn* 12:20-24).

If we take the phrase in the interrogative sense, we can understand that it is now the hour of the first manifestation of Jesus' glory, but not the hour of his definitive manifestation, which will be achieved through the exultation of the cross and his ascension into heaven.

So, what does Mary do? In the parallel passages, the Synoptic Gospels do not tell us how Mary reacted. The fourth Gospel does tell us: Mary submitted perfectly to the invitation of Jesus; she does not ask anything of him but, without turning to him again, she turns to the servants and says to them: "Do whatever he tells you" (*Jn* 2:5). The translations often have: "Do what he will tell you", which suggests that Mary knew intuitively what Jesus would do. In any case, she invites the servants to perfect docility: "Whatever he tells you to do, do it". She leaves the initiative completely to Jesus. Mary not only consents personally to the words of Jesus and accepts a change of relationship, but she also invites others to surrender themselves to him. Mary abandons the first level of relationship with Jesus and establishes herself on a new level. With her characteristic docility, she again shows that she serves the Lord. She becomes the mother of Christ in a new manner, according to Jesus' declaration in the Synoptics: "For whoever does the will of my Father in Heaven, is my brother and sister and mother" (*Mt* 12:50). Mary accepts the will of God and at the same time, leads others to manifest the same generous submission. In this way, Mary becomes the mother of Jesus in a two-fold sense because now she is also the mother of Jesus' disciples: those who do what Jesus asks.

It seems to me that we can admire the great availability of Mary and that it is better not to try to give devotional explanations to this episode, which, to a greater or lesser degree, deviate from the corresponding orientation of the fourth Gospel. In the fourth Gospel, it is always Jesus who takes the initiative for miracles; there is no request for miracles on the part of other people. The interpretation that I propose, seems to me to correspond better to a truly profound devotion to Mary. Mary is our mother who teaches us true docility to the Lord.

Now let us imagine the impossible for a moment; let us imagine that Mary was a possessive mother, jealous, as in the case of a mother who does not allow her children, even as adults and married men and women, to follow their own way, thus provoking so many family dramas. If Mary were like this, she would have been very put out by Jesus' response. She would have considered it an intolerable lack of respect and would not have accepted a change in their relationship. Instead of putting herself at the service of Jesus' mission, she would have become an obstacle to it. Clearly, this hypothesis is completely unrealistic in Mary's case, but unfortunately for others, it has been a reality. There was, in fact, a part of the chosen people, namely: the Pharisees, the Scribes and the High Priests who originally found themselves in the same position as Mary in relation to Jesus – that is, in a position of authority. Jesus presented himself to them as a prophet sent by God in order to establish a New Covenant. Jesus taught "... as one who had authority and not as the Scribes" (*Mk* 1:22). He required a change of relationship. However, they did not accept him and they opposed his Messianic action and his mission even to the extent of having him condemned to death.

This Gospel episode confronts us with a choice between two opposed spiritual attitudes: that of Mary's docility and that of those who do not want to accept any change of relationship when Jesus proposes it. The Apostle Paul, at the beginning of the parenetic[5] part of the Letter to the Romans gives us to understand that we cannot rest, in a definitive way, at any particular level of the spiritual life or in any particular kind of pastoral ministry. Now and then, our Lord asks us for a change of relationship. St Paul tells us: "Be transformed by the renewal of your mind, that you may prove what is the will of God, what is good and acceptable and perfect" (*Rm* 12:2). I emphasize, "Be transformed by the renewal of your mind". In the New Testament, the will of God cannot be a fixed law written on stone; it is a creative will and if we want to correspond to the will of God, we must correspond to this creative movement, especially when the Lord asks us for a change of relationship. Through external circumstances, through decisions of other persons or even in other ways, for example, by means of a spiritual desolation that leads us to question our way of understanding our relationship with God, Christ puts to us the same question that he put to Mary: "What is your current relationship with me? Does it correspond to the current stage of your vocation or of your mission? You cannot be content with your past relationship, however good as it might have been. This relationship must now progress; it must correspond to a new stage of your spiritual and apostolic life. At such times, we may have the impression that the Lord wants to take away from us what we

---

5 teaching or doctrinal part

have, but the Lord's intention is, in fact, positive. He wants us to move on to a level of purer love: one that is more profound and more fruitful, so that the Messianic marriage feast between him and us may be brought to fulfillment. It is a wonderful grace to recognize the moment in which the Lord responds to us as abruptly as he responded to Mary at Cana; it is a wonderful grace to understand the positive intention of the Lord, which is always a progression of love.

10
Christ, Mediator of the New Covenant in the Last Supper (Mt 26:26-28)

At the wedding feast at Cana, as we have seen, Jesus changed water into wine. This sign anticipated the Last Supper, at which Jesus changed wine into his own blood. The wedding feast of Cana, a nuptial covenant, pre-announced the institution of the New Covenant. At the Last Supper, Jesus instituted this New Covenant, saying: "This cup is the New Covenant in my blood" (*Lk* 22:19; *1 Co* 11:25). In this way, he revealed, as mediator of the New Covenant, that he is in fact its High Priest. I propose to you, therefore, that we meditate this evening on the institution of the Eucharist, an inestimable treasure for which we can attest an ever-increasing admiration and veneration.

We know well, that the Eucharist is an astonishing gift of love. Perhaps we do not know well enough that the institution of the Eucharist was a victory of love. It was an extraordinary victory of love over evil and death. This is due to the fact that all the accounts of the Last Supper placed the Eucharist in the context of the passion of Jesus and more precisely with the betrayal of Judas. St Paul, in his First Letter to the Corinthians, declares: "The Lord Jesus on the night when he was betrayed took bread and when he had given thanks, he broke it, and said, 'This is my body which is for you'" (*1 Co* 11:23-24). The Gospels reveal that before instituting the Eucharist, Jesus was aware of the betrayal;

he said: "Truly, I say to you, one of you will betray me" (*Mt* 26:21; *Mk* 14:18). Therefore, the chain of events that would bring Jesus to condemnation and to infamous death on the cross has already been put into motion. The Lord was aware of this. He knew that his ministry, a most generous dedication to God and to the brethren, would be brutally interrupted by betrayal which was the most odious sin and the one most contrary to the Covenant's dynamism. However, he could still act freely; within a few hours he would be arrested and tried; then he would no longer be free, and still less when he would be nailed to the cross. So what is his reaction?

What would be the expected reaction in such a scandalous situation? Let us see the reaction of the prophet Jeremiah. There is a striking similarity between the life of Jeremiah and that of Jesus. Warned by the Lord of a plot made against him, Jeremiah exclaims: "But, oh Lord of hosts, who judges righteously, who tries the heart and the mind, let me see thy vengeance upon them, for I have committed my cause to thee" (*Jr* 11:20; 20:12). In another passage, Jeremiah specifies what the vengeance must be: "Give heed to me, oh Lord, and hearken to my plea. Deliver up their children to famine, give them over to the power of the sword, let their wives become childless and widowed. May their men meet death by pestilence, their youths be slain by the sword in battle. Forgive not their iniquity" (*Jr* 18:19; 21;23). This is what you might call a "normal" reaction in such a situation of scandalous injustice. On the contrary, we can note that Jeremiah's attitude already constitutes a certain progress in regard to the instinctive human reaction that would be to take up one's sword in personal vengeance. Jeremiah, however, entrusts the vengeance to God. At this point, it is a victory over violent impulse. Nevertheless, Jesus achieves a far more radical and positive victory. He overcomes his discomfort and instead of renouncing, like Jeremiah, his attitude of generosity, he takes it to the extreme: "Having loved his own who were in the world, he loved them to the end" (*Jn* 13:1).

Jesus anticipates his own death. He makes it present in the bread that is broken, which becomes his own body and in the wine poured out which becomes his own blood. He transforms his death into a covenant sacrifice for the good of all. It is not possible to imagine a greater generosity than this. It is not possible to imagine a more radical transformation than this event. When the Eucharist is spoken of, there is usually an insistence on the transformation of the bread into the body of Christ and of the wine into his blood, that is, transubstantiation, the importance of which is clearly decisive. Without it, there would be no Sacrament. However, another transformation, no less extraordinary, generally goes unnoticed; in fact, in a very specific sense, it is more important for our life: it is the transformation of an event that is broken in mid-act so as to establish communion with God and the brothers. It is the transformation of blood, criminally spilt by enemies, into blood of the Covenant. This transformation is truly stupendous. It is an extraordinary victory of love.

In the Old Testament, death was an event of radical and definitive brokenness with men and with God. However, we no longer understand it in this way because Jesus has overturned the meaning of death in the Last Supper. We know that death breaks physical ties between persons. It is not possible to communicate with a dead person. He or she cannot be spoken to and there can no longer be personal and reciprocal contact. This is why we are sad and grieve. However, we also know that our deceased rests spiritually in Christ; the rupture is not total. In the Old Testament, it seemed to be total.

In the Old Testament mentality, death was especially the rupture of the relationship with God. This was its most tremendous aspect for religious people. Death was understood to be a punishment for sin. It was the final consequence of sin, the extreme level of the rupture between human persons and God. In the Old Testament, when they considered death, they considered this tremendous rupture. Struck down by a mortal illness, King Hezekiah exclaims: "I shall not see the Lord in the land of the living" (*Is* 38:11). The Lord is seen to be in the land of the living. He is not seen in *Sheol,* the land of the dead. The people of the Old Testament perceived a violent contrast between the living God and the deceased person and they deemed any positive relationship between them to be impossible. In Psalm 87/88, the one praying turns to God with these words: "My life draws near to Sheol. I am reckoned among those who go down to the pit; I am a man who has no strength, like one forsaken among the dead, like the slain that lie in the grave, like those whom thou dost remember no more, for they are cut off from thy hand" (*Ps* 87/88:5-6). God has forgotten the dead; the rupture is complete. According to the understanding of the Old Testament, as you know well, the dead ended up in *Sheol,* that is, a dark, subterranean place where they had a shadowy existence unworthy of man and even more unworthy of God.

This twofold aspect of the rupture provoked by death became even more tragic when it concerned the death of a condemned person. Even the death of an honest person causes grief and sadness. We wish that the person had not died. On the other hand, the one condemned to death is rejected by the society that no longer wants him and condemns him precisely to make a complete and definitive rupture with him. Among the chosen people, condemnation occurred according to God's Law. So, the condemned were considered to have been be cursed by God. It is precisely this situation of complete rupture that Jesus must face at the Last Supper. St Paul did not hesitate to say that Christ has become a "curse" since it was written: "cursed be every one who hangs on a tree" (*Ga* 3:13; *Dt* 21:23). Jesus assumes this situation and makes it the occasion of extreme love; he makes it an instrument of communion with God and with the brethren and a means of establishing the Covenant. More contrary circumstances to the establishment of the Covenant could not be imagined. Jesus knows that he will be betrayed. He knows that he will be abandoned by all his disciples, denied by Peter, arrested, falsely accused, condemned with the worst of the unjust and killed. It is precisely these cruel and unjust events that he makes present and anticipates at the Last Supper, transforming it into a gift of love in the offering of the Covenant.

If we really ponder it seriously, this reality would have to leave us profoundly stupefied. It seems to me that we do not give enough importance to the extraordinary transformation worked by Jesus in this moment and to the generosity of heart by which he has conceived and effected such a transformation. We do not give enough importance to the dynamism of victorious love that we receive when we celebrate the Eucharist and give Holy Communion. It is a dynamism that enables us to easily overcome all the obstacles to love. It should give us the strength to transform those obstacles into opportunities for progress in love. We should feel so much shame for our lack of love and for the times we have allowed our love to be defeated.

A covenant must have two dimensions: the vertical dimension of the relationship with God and the horizontal dimension of the relationship with the brethren. These are the two dimensions of the cross. They are very significant and are at the centre of the heart of Christ, which unites these two dimensions. In the establishment of the Covenant of Sinai, the most apparent dimension was the vertical one. We read in Exodus that Moses, "took the Book of the Covenant and read it in the hearing of the people, and they said, 'All that the Lord has spoken we will do, and we will be obedient' and Moses took the blood and threw it upon the people and said, 'Behold the blood of the Covenant which the Lord has made with you in accordance with all these words'" (*Ex* 24:7-8). This was the vertical dimension between the people and God.

In the Last Supper, on the contrary, the most apparent dimension is the horizontal dimension of the self-donation to the brethren. The context is a meal taken together. It is a context of human brotherhood. Every meal taken together has this meaning of a union between persons, reciprocal acceptance, friendship and fraternal relationships. In this context of a meal taken together, Jesus offers his own body as food and his own blood as drink: "This is my body which is given for you … This cup which is poured out for you is the New Covenant in my blood" (*Lk* 22:19-20). Therefore, we find ourselves faced with a fraternal communion that is expressed in the most intimate and perfect way possible. The blood of the Covenant is not sprinkled as it was in the first Covenant of Sinai, but is given as drink. The outcome is a reciprocal imminence: "He who eats my flesh and drinks my blood abides in me, and I in him" (*Jn* 6:56). It would not be possible to achieve a more intimate covenant. This aspect of profound communion between Jesus and the disciples present at the Last Supper is not regained at Calvary. There, only the complete rupture is manifested. Jesus dies on the cross, rejected by the multitude. Thanks to the Last Supper, we know that he dies for the multitude and establishes the Covenant with God.

The vertical dimension of the Last Supper is less evident but it is essential; it conditions the horizontal: There cannot be a true union among the brethren if there is not a relationship with the Father. Where is the vertical dimension manifested? It is manifested in a single word: «ευχαριστησας» – "*eucharistesas*", "And when he had given thanks…" (*Lk* 22:19). These words express the thanksgiving that Jesus pronounced twice, first over the bread and then over the chalice. It concerns a prayer of extreme importance. The Church has understood it well because it has called the Sacrament "Eucharist", a Greek word, which means "thanksgiving". The Eucharist is the Sacrament of thanksgiving.

Throughout his life, Jesus often spontaneously assumed the filial attitude of grateful love. It is an attitude that corresponds to his condition as Son: As Son, he receives everything from his Father. So his normal reaction is to receive the Father's gifts with filial gratitude. The Gospels refer us to some instances where Jesus had publicly offered thanks to the Father. This leads us to take two aspects into consideration since they are related to the Eucharist. It concerns two situations in which giving thanks to God would not normally come to mind: the first is a situation of deficiency and the second is a situation of grief. The situation of deficiency is one that immediately precedes the multiplication of the loaves: there are thousands of hungry people in a deserted place and Jesus has only seven loaves at hand. It does not seem to be the time to rejoice or to offer thanks; what is necessary is lacking. In the Book of Exodus, in similar situations when food was lacking, the people certainly did not rejoice. They murmured and rebelled (cf. *Ex* 16:2-3). Jesus, however, rejoices and gives thanks to the Father (*Mt* 15:36; *Mk* 8:6) and, in this way, initiates the multiplication of the loaves. With his thanksgiving, he has opened the way to the Father's generosity. The situation of grief is one that occurs immediately after the death of Lazarus. Jesus is taken to the tomb of his friend. He orders it to be opened and in front of the open sepulchre, he turns to the Father with this completely unexpected prayer in the circumstances, "Father, I thank thee that thou has heard me" (*Jn* 11:41).

In the Last Supper, Jesus offers thanks. This is not a moment of facile joy. It is a tragic situation; it is one of betrayal. Jesus offers thanks. At first sight, this thanksgiving is presented as an ordinary fact of daily life, like a prayer at the beginning of meals. When the Apostles hear Jesus' thanksgiving, the meaning that they perceive is this: "Father, I give you thanks for this bread that you have given me, with which you generously nourish all your creatures. I give you thanks for this wine. It is a symbol of your love, with which you give joy to the hearts of men". However, Jesus himself knows exactly he is going to say and do in the next moment. He knows very well that this meal is not going to remain an ordinary meal and that this bread and this wine will not remain a material bread and wine. In offering thanks, he knows that the

Father offers him the possibility of an incomparably greater gift which is more substantial and more generous, namely: the gift of himself, so that Jesus may communicate the divine love, the divine life to men.

The first aspect of the Eucharist, however, is not Jesus' gift to us. It is his gift to the Father. In the discourse of the bread of life, Jesus had said: "Truly, truly, I say to you, it was not Moses that gave you the bread from heaven; my Father gives you the true bread from heaven" (*Jn* 6:32). Jesus is fully aware that the gift that he gives comes from the Father. He does not claim to take the initiative, but offers thanks to the Father who gives him the capacity to transmit this gift: "I give thanks to the Father because, through this bread which I have in my hands, I will become bread for the life of the world. I offer you thanks for having given me a body that I can transform into spiritual food and for having given me my blood that I can share and transform into the drink of the Covenant. Above all, I give you thanks for having given me a heart that is full of love, for it ardently desires to give this gift". The Eucharist is the gift of the Father who gives an excellent food to his children. The Church receives the Eucharist as the gift of the Father. This aspect is regularly expressed in the liturgical prayers after Communion that have a surprising dimension. After Communion, it would seem to be the time to give thanks to Jesus who has given himself to us. The church, however, offers thanks to the Father. The prayers speak of the Father who has received us at his table, the Father who has nourished us with the body and blood of his Son, that is, the Eucharist, the gift of the Father.

In the discourse on the bread of life, Jesus had said: "And the bread which I shall give for the life of the world is my flesh" (*Jn* 6:51). At the Last Supper, Jesus does not limit his gaze to the small group surrounding him but says to the disciples: "Do this in remembrance of me". He is thinking of so many others. In this way, we realize that His thanksgiving is the origin of a new multiplication. This time, it is not a multiplication of loaves in the plural, but of bread; a unique bread that is himself.   It is a multiplication that is still more marvellous and significant than that which happened in the desert.   In effect, the aim of this last multiplication was not so much the feeding of some thousands of people as the prefiguring of the multiplication of the Eucharistic Bread.   The multiplication of loaves was a sign.   Jesus explicitly says so the day after the event (*Jn* 6:26).   At the Last Supper, when Jesus gives thanks to the Father, he thinks of this new and infinite distribution: "Father, I unite myself to you with immense gratitude because you make me the living bread that is given for the life of the world, infinitely multiplied for all people".

If we compare Jesus' thanksgiving at the Last Supper with his thanksgiving at Lazarus' tomb, we can immediately see the difference.   In one case, we see a prayer made at the opening to a sepulchre.   In the other case, we see a meal taken together in the intimacy of the cenacle.   However, on deeper reflection, we are able to perceive a profound similarity between these two prayers.   In both cases, Jesus must face death and conquer it.   In the first case, he has to face and conquer the death of his friend Lazarus.   In the second case, he has to face and conquer his own death.   In both cases, Jesus gives thanks to the Father for the victory.   We can say that, at the Last Supper, Jesus expressed the same sentiments which he had expressed in front of Lazarus' tomb when he had said: "Father, I thank that thee that thou hast heard me" (*Jn* 11:41).   He was sure of having been heard by the Father and of having won the victory over the death of his friend. Similarly, at the Last Supper, he fully gives thanks to the Father for the victory which he is about to achieve over death itself: "Father, I give you thanks because I know in advance that you have given the victory over death for me and for all.   I give you thanks because you now put into my heart all the strength of your love, which is capable of conquering death and transforming it into an occasion of the most perfect and complete gift of myself. Thanks to the strength of this love that comes from you, my body will become the bread of life. My blood that is poured out will become the source of communion, the blood of the Covenant. All will be able to receive this gift. Father, I give you thanks for this marvellous possibility". Inasmuch as his thanksgiving is an anticipation of the victory, this prayer constitutes an exceptional revelation of Jesus' interior life and of his filial union with the Father in the most absolute trust.

At the same time, this thanksgiving constitutes an extremely efficacious action because it is decisive for all the events that follow: the institution of the Eucharist, the passion, the resurrection and the establishment of the New Covenant. Everything depends on this thanksgiving because everything depends on the generous gift of the Father that is received by Jesus with perfect gratitude.

We can now briefly make a comparison with the Old Testament, in order to give a better account of the newness of the Eucharist as a sacrifice of thanksgiving. The Old Testament knew this sacrifice of thanksgiving very well, which it called in Hebrew, *toda*, a word that has the idea of "acknowledgement". The custom was very simple: the one who is found to be in danger of death invokes God with intense prayer and promises to offer thanksgiving if he or she is preserved from death. If this condition comes true, the person then brings, at the time of offering and in the midst of the festive assembly, the thanksgiving sacrifice that concludes with a communion and sacrificial meal in which all eat of the immolated victim. The custom is often represented in the Psalms. In Jesus' case, the surprising thing is that he has put the thanksgiving first, which normally comes at the end. At the Last Supper, we know well that Jesus anticipated his death, even making it present in anticipation; perhaps we do not reflect enough on the fact that Christ also anticipated the final thanksgiving for the victory over death, which he obtained precisely through his death. He has put first what is usually the last element, namely: thanksgiving for the communion meal. He has put it at the beginning because it is the fundamental and even the decisive element.

All these observations help us to understand the depth of the mystery and the strength of love that has achieved such a transformation. The love that comes from the Father passes through the heart of Christ and transforms a tragic and scandalous event into a source of infinite grace. When we celebrate the Eucharist and when we receive Holy Communion, we welcome this intense dynamism of love, which is capable of transforming all events into an occasion of love's victory. We must become more conscious of this.

11
The Sacrifice of Christ
(Hb 9:11-12)

We now return to the Letter to the Hebrews. I propose to you that we meditate upon the sacrifice of Christ, which is presented in the central part of this preaching, that is, in chapters 8 and 9. The author presents here a very substantial doctrine of Christ's sacrifice. In today's parlance, the word sacrifice has negative connotations; it signifies a privation. Instead, its religious meaning is very positive and our author enables us to see this.

Christ's sacrifice comprises the whole Paschal Mystery, that is, his death and his glorification. The glorification certainly belongs to the sacrifice of Christ. It is the positive perspective that the Letter to the Hebrews offers us. "To sacrifice" does not, in fact, mean to deprive; it means to make sacred, just as "to sanctify" means to make holy and as "to simplify" means to make simple. Therefore, to sacrifice is a very positive and fruitful act that places immense value on the offering. The sacrifice of Christ comprises his glorification. Without his glorification, it would be incomplete; it would not have established the New Covenant because Christ would not have reached God; nor would he have achieved the link between our misery and God's holiness. Christ has become the High Priest of the New Covenant because, thanks to his passion and his glorification, he has passed from the earthly to the heavenly Sanctuary and so has acquired the capacity to introduce us into full communion with the Father and into perfect fraternal communion.

To help us understand better the religious value of the passion and resurrection of Christ, the author expresses the Paschal Mystery in a cultural language and relates it to old priestly worship, thus demonstrating the similarity and at the same time the great difference.   We have already observed that when Jeremiah announced the New Covenant, he did not explain how it would be established. Instead, the author of the Letter to the Hebrews has been very attentive to this point. He has understood that the Covenant must necessarily be founded on an act of mediation that would be capable of removing the obstacles and establishing communion between God and us.   In establishing the New Covenant, a sacrificial mediation was needed, just like in the Old Covenant. However, this act of mediation would have to be very different from the ancient attempts at mediation, which had been inefficacious. This act of mediation is the sacrificial offering of Christ.   The author deepens this theme in the central section of his preaching, precisely in chapters 8 and 9. These chapters are characterized by the intimate link that the author establishes between worship and the Covenant. He introduces the topic of worship at the beginning of chapter 8, where he affirms that Christ is the liturgical minister of the Sanctuary and has offered a sacrifice. Then he introduces the theme of the Covenant in connection with the worship in verse 6, saying: "Christ has obtained a ministry which is as much more excellent than the old as the Covenant he mediates is better". The author then cites and briefly comments on the beautiful oracle of Jeremiah that announces the New Covenant (*Hb* 8:8-12). At the beginning of chapter 9, the author returns to the theme of worship, saying that the first Covenant had regulations for worship and an earthly sanctuary. He describes the old worship right up till verse 10 and then contra-poses to this worship the sacrifice of Christ, his offering and the new worship. In verse 15 of chapter 9, he takes up again the theme of the Covenant saying that, with his offering, Christ has become "the Mediator of a New Covenant".

He enlarges this until verse 23 and concludes with a theme of worship from verses 24 to 28. In these two chapters you see that we have a continuous alternation between worship and covenant, which closely links these two realities.

This link constitutes a novelty with respect to the Old Testament. Indeed, the Book of Leviticus, when it treats of the worship and of the prescriptions for sacrifices, does not present the theme of covenant. On the other hand, the oracle of Jeremiah, as I have already mentioned, speaks much of covenant, but says nothing at all about worship. Instead, for the author of the Letter to the Hebrews, worship and covenant are intimately united. This corresponds to his idea of the priest as a man of mediation. The offering is made to establish the Covenant and it is not possible to establish a covenant without an offering.

The Old Covenant was incomplete because it was established on an inadequate worship. In chapter 9, the author analyzes this worship so as to demonstrate that it did not achieve its aim. He begins by saying: "Now even the first Covenant had regulations for worship and an earthly sanctuary" (*Hb* 9:1). The Sanctuary of the Old Covenant was earthly; that is, humans fabricated it. An earthly sanctuary is not a suitable instrument for obtaining communion with God. The Old Testament already asserted this (cf. *1 K* 8:27; *Is* 66:1). In the following verses, the author does not refer to the Temple of Jerusalem but to the Tent because he wants to establish his discourse on the Law of Moses, that is, on the Pentateuch, which says nothing of the Temple. It described only the Tent of the Book of Exodus. The author then describes the Tent, which was divided into two parts: the first part was called "the first Tent". The first Tent was the only way to enter into the second and this is an important concept, as we shall see. The second was considered to be the dwelling place of God but it was not really. A first Tent, fabricated by man, could only introduce one to a second Tent, which was also made by man; so God could not really dwell there. The author then recalls the order of ceremonies, according to which the simple priests would enter each time into the first Tent to perform the ceremonies of worship. However, only the High Priest would enter the second Tent and that only once a year and never without carrying the blood which he would offer for sins (*Hb* 9:6-7).

This was the ancient system. It was a system of successive separations in order that one might prudently approach the holiness of God. However, true contact with God was not established in this way. The author says that with these rites, "The Holy Spirit indicates that the way into the sanctuary is not yet opened as long as the outer Tent is still standing" (*RSV Hb* 9:8). The translations usually have: "The way was still not opened", because we usually refer to a way as being opened or closed. However, the author did not say "opened"; he said "manifested" or "revealed", which is different. In other words, the true way was simply not known. The first or outer Tent was not the way into the true Sanctuary; what this way would be was still unknown, it had not yet been manifested.

They had no way of passing through the true way, because they were offering, says the author, "gifts and sacrifices…which cannot perfect the conscience of the worshipper" (*Hb* 9:9). Speaking in this way, the author expresses an idea concerning the aim of sacrifice. Sacrifices are spontaneously understood to be gifts offered to God in order to obtain his favours. The concept of sacrifice is based on what happens in human relationships. The aim is to change God's dispositions. For example, we see the sacrifices of Noah in the Book of Genesis: Noah leaves the ark, builds an altar and offers holocausts to the Lord who, when he had smelt the pleasing odour, said, "I will never again curse the ground because of man" (*Gn* 8:21). God's disposition was changed by Noah's sacrifice. The author, however, says that the aim of the sacrifice is to change man's dispositions, not God's. Its aim is "To make perfect the conscience of the worshipper", that is, to purify his heart and make him docile to God. Clearly, the ancient sacrifices did not have such a capacity. How could the cadavers of immolated animals perfect the conscience of a human person? There is no relationship between these two realities. So, the system of sacrificial offering in the Old Testament was inadequate. As long as man's heart was unchanged, it was impossible for him to have an authentic relationship with God. Therefore, the aim of sacrifice could not be achieved. As the author points out, the Old Testament worship only dealt with food and drink and various ablutions. All of these were external rites, that is, literally "rites of the flesh", as he says; they were prescriptions of merely ritual purity that could do nothing to change man's heart.

As you can see, the author makes a very strong critique of the ancient worship and of its incapacity for establishing an authentic mediation. In the Old Testament, there were some very praiseworthy things: the religious aspiration was expressed with generous offerings. This, among other things, was positive. However, a religious aspiration is not enough to change the conscience of a sinner. To put sinful man in true contact with God, there must be an efficacious mediation. The sinner must be helped by a mediator who is not himself a sinner and who will open for him the way of communion with God. This is the problem of the Covenant.

When Christ came, he manifested the way, established communication and founded the Covenant. The author triumphantly affirms this in chapter 9, verses 11 and following. I translate literally: "Christ instead, having come as High Priest of the good things still to come, through the greater and more perfect Tent not built by human hands, that is, not belonging to this creation, and not with the blood of goats and calves but with his own blood, entered once and for all into the Sanctuary, having obtained an eternal redemption". In the language of worship, this sentence presents the whole Paschal Mystery of Christ: his passion, resurrection and ascension. The Sanctuary into which Christ enters is not material but heavenly, as the author later on specifies (cf. *Hb* 9:24). By entering the true Sanctuary, Christ has re-established communication between man and God: he has opened for us the way to God. Better still, he himself has become the way. In the fourth Gospel, Jesus says: "I am the Way" (*Jn* 14:6). He has become the way that achieves the Paschal Mystery. As the Son of God, Jesus had no personal need of sacrifice. However, he did have this need in his human nature. By means of his generous offering, he obtained the transformation of his own human nature that it might, in this way, be introduced into heavenly intimacy with God. By what means has God re-established communication? The author speaks of two means, in a parallel way. He cleverly exploits the Greek preposition «δια», which means "through" but can also mean "by means of": Christ has entered into the true Sanctuary "by means of the greatest Tent … and by means of his blood".

The second means is very easy to interpret. The blood of Christ clearly signifies the offering of his life; it indicates his own violent death that is transformed into an offering of love. The blood of Christ is contra-posed to that of goats and calves. These are unconscious victims. Here we can admire the generosity of Christ our High Priest. He has not searched the flock for a lamb without blemish, as the levitical ritual required so that it could be offered in sacrifice. Rather, he has offered his own life, facing suffering and death in perfect obedience to the salvific will of the Father and with a most generous love for us men. His blood expresses this aspect of a violent death now transformed into an offering of filial obedience and fraternal solidarity.

So we can now see what the blood represents; but what does the author intend when he speaks of "the greater and more perfect Tent" on which he firmly insists? Exegetes seem to be quite perplexed over the identification of this Tent. The most common explanation is that this Tent represents the lower heavens. Christ has had to go through the lower heavens in order to penetrate with his human nature the divine heaven. But this explanation is not at all satisfactory since the "lower heavens" represents a way that was always known. However, the new way was not known; it had not yet been manifested. Also, the lower heavens formed part of this creation, as the author had said in chapter 1. They will perish with this creation (1:10-12). He expresses this again in 12:26-27. Furthermore, the author's parallelism between the Tent and the blood, which is very close in the Greek phrase, is not explained at all if the Tent is identified with the lower heavens. The heavens and the blood are not parallel realities.

St John Chrysostom has proposed a more profound interpretation that adheres more to the text and is richer from the spiritual and doctrinal points of view. He affirmed that "the greater and more perfect Tent that does not belong to this creation" is the body of Christ. However, it is necessary to be specific and say: "the glorified body of Christ". This is because, prior to his glorification, the body of Christ belonged to this creation, for it was a body like ours. By means of the glorification, it has become the new creation. According to the Letter to the Hebrews, the new way to enter into intimacy with God is the human nature of Christ, which is transformed and glorified in his sacrifice. The parallelism with the blood then is perfectly understood. Christ has entered into divine intimacy by means of his glorified body and by means of his blood. This is perfectly coherent; the parallel between the body and the blood corresponds to the two aspects of the offering; Christ has poured out his own blood, that is, he has generously offered his own life and with this offering, he has obtained the transformation of his human nature; he has renewed it, rendering it worthy of entering into intimacy with God. His human nature has become the way that leads into the glorious intimacy of God. This way was not manifested at first. It was completely unknown; it has only been manifested in the Paschal Mystery of Christ.

This concept of the Letter to the Hebrews corresponds to a teaching of the Gospels but with greater precision. In the fourth

Gospel, as I have already mentioned, when the Jews asked Jesus with what authority he had scattered the money-changers from the Temple, Jesus answers: "Destroy this Temple and in three days I will raise it up" (*Jn* 2:19). The evangelist comments: "But he spoke of the Temple of his body" (2:21). The mystery of the death and resurrection of Jesus is therefore presented in the fourth Gospel as the mystery of an earthly Sanctuary that is transformed in three days and becomes the heavenly Sanctuary by means of the passion and glorification. In the synoptic Gospels, the only accusation that is expressed against Jesus during the process before the Sanhedrin is precisely that of having declared: "I will destroy this Temple that is made with hands and in three days, I will build another, not made with hands" (*Mk* 14:58). The author of the Letter to the Hebrews has reclaimed the same qualification for the Tent: it is not made by human hands. The accusation is false, as the synoptics say, because Jesus had never said, "I will destroy". Jesus had predicted the destruction of the Temple and announced the construction of a new Sanctuary. The glorified body of Christ is therefore the true Tent; he builds for us the way to enter into intimacy with God. Through that Tent, Christ has presented himself before the Father in heaven on our behalf.

The original contribution of the Letter to the Hebrews consists in the precise distinction between the two parts of the sacred place: the way and the dwelling place of God; or the vestibule and the Holy of Holies. The dwelling place of God is forever in heaven; there was no need for its reconstruction. However, a new vestibule was needed, that is, a suitable *way* into this heavenly dwelling place which is not made by human hands. This *way* is the glorified body of Christ, and it is said to be "more perfect" than the ancient Sanctuary because the humanity of Christ has been made perfect by means of his suffering. The author has already said this in preceding chapters (*Hb* 2:10; 5:8-9). On the other hand, this Tent is "greater" than the ancient Sanctuary because, with his offering, Christ has obtained that all believers can become members of his body, as St Paul explicitly quotes: "Now you are the body of Christ and individually members of it" (*1 Co* 12:27). "Through the greater and more perfect Tent", that is, by means of his glorified body, "Christ has entered once and for all into the heavenly Sanctuary". Before the passion, his body belonged to this creation; it was a body like ours, but through his passion, it has become a new creation, which has been inaugurated with his resurrection. St Paul affirms, "If anyone is in Christ, he is a new creation" (*2 Co* 5:17); *a fortiori*, Christ himself is the new creation. Therefore, the two means that re-establish communication between God and us and establish the New Covenant are the body and the blood of Christ. We receive this in the Eucharist; we can enter into intimacy with God as we are made part of the glorified body of Christ and this has been made possible by the shedding of his blood, that is, by his most generous offering of himself in the passion.

In this way, the Letter to the Hebrews offers us the priestly and sacrificial way of understanding the Paschal Mystery of Christ. St Paul had already suggested the sacrificial interpretation when he said, "Christ, our paschal lamb, has been sacrificed" (*1 Co* 5:7). The Letter to the Ephesians is still more explicit when it says that: "Christ loved us and gave himself up for us, a fragrant offering and sacrifice to God" (*Eph* 5:2). The author of the Letter to the Hebrews profoundly exploits this thought and so introduces us into the dynamism of Christ's sacrifice. It is an intense dynamism that starts from our human misery and unites it to the heavenly intimacy of God. We are privileged because we can always profit from this intense dynamism.

12
The Holy Spirit in the Sacrifice of Christ
(Hb 9:14)

L et us continue our meditation on Christ's sacrifice which is presented in the Letter to the Hebrews, a sacrifice that comprises the passion and the resurrection; let us now see its relationship to the Holy Spirit, thanks to a very important phrase of the Letter to the Hebrews which follows the passage on which we have just been meditating. In verses 13 and 14 of chapter 9, the author, in lengthy explanation, gives an account of the efficacy of Christ's blood for the establishment of the New Covenant. He begins with a reference to the ancient sacrifices, so as then to provide an argument a *fortiori*:

> For if the sprinkling of defiled persons with the blood of goats and bulls and with the ashes of a heifer sanctifies for the purification of the flesh, how much more shall the blood of Christ, who through the eternal Spirit offered himself without blemish to God, purify your conscience from dead works to serve the living God. Therefore he is the Mediator of a New Covenant...

This is a very rich passage from a doctrinal point of view. It enables us to deepen the mystery of the passion and glorification of Christ and gives us to understand that the blood poured out by Christ has become the blood of the New Covenant because it was the expression of a perfect personal offering, made under the impulse of the Holy Spirit.

In the old worship, external gifts and sacrifices were offered, cadavers of immolated animals which conferred the ritual purity for external worship but could not establish an authentic covenant with God because they were incapable of having an influence over the conscience of the person. Christ, instead, offered himself without blemish to God under the impulse of the Holy Spirit. His sacrifice was a personal offering and not an external offering. It was an offering of his whole human nature. The statement that Christ *offered* himself completes the passive aspect expressed in chapter 5 where the author says that: "Jesus *was made* perfect" which is passive. However, Jesus is never content with a passive acceptance of the will of the Father. Throughout his life, he shows himself to be full of initiative; he faced difficulties and resolutely took the road for Jerusalem (*Lk* 9:53). In Gethsemane, he voluntarily allowed himself to be arrested, even forbidding Peter to defend him.

Christ "offered himself", while the ancient High Priest could not offer himself. He was neither worthy nor capable. He was not worthy because he was a sinner and so he must offer immolated animals *for* himself; he could not be a victim pleasing to God because, according to Leviticus, the condition was that the victim be "without blemish" (*Lv* 1:3; 10) and the High Priest was not without stain of sin. On the other hand, he was not capable of offering himself because, being a sinner, he did not have in himself all the strength of love necessary for offering himself to God. Jesus, instead, was a worthy victim and a capable priest. He was a worthy Victim because he had perfect moral and religious integrity; he was truly "without blemish" (9:14). As the author says, he was "holy, blameless, unstained" (*Hb* 7:26). He was a capable priest because he was full of the power of the Holy Spirit.

The newness that we find here consists precisely in the role attributed to the Spirit in the offering of Christ. The Gospels frequently mention the Holy Spirit in relation to Jesus: firstly, for his conception, then in his baptism and in the course of his ministry; however, they do not mention the Holy Spirit in the passion. The Letter to the Hebrews, instead, says that the Paschal Mystery of Christ was a mystery effected under the impulse of the Holy Spirit.

It is true that the author does not specifically say "Holy Spirit"; he says "the eternal Spirit" which is the only such expression in the Bible and, as such, has had various interpretations. Nevertheless, the single truly coherent interpretation is that proposed by Greek patristics, according to which the eternal Spirit is another way of designating the Holy Spirit. Only God is eternal, therefore, the eternal Spirit is the Spirit of God. It is the Holy Spirit.

The adjective "eternal" was not chosen without reason. With that, the author wanted to express the value of Christ's offering which gives us the possibility of obtaining an "eternal redemption" as he has said in the preceding verse (9:9-12); he will say in a following verse (9:15) that it was made to procure for us "an eternal inheritance" and finally, at the end of the Letter (13:20), he will say that it was offered in order to establish "an eternal Covenant". Only the power of the eternal Spirit could communicate to Christ the necessary impulse to achieve an offering of such great efficacy. It is an offering capable of establishing a truly new and eternal Covenant. With this interpretation, the sacrifice is situated in a beautiful trinitarian perspective which we take up again in a prayer of the Mass recited by the priest before communion: *"Lord Jesus Christ, Son of the living God, by the will of the Father and by the work of the Holy Spirit, your death brought life to the world…"*.

In this text, (Hb 9:14), the event of Calvary is implicitly contra-posed to the rites of the Old Testament, which the author has called "regulations for the body" (*Hb* 9:10), that is, rites in which the Holy Spirit was not operative and which could not then procure true purity or true holiness. St John Chrysostom suggests that the author wanted to show that the Holy Spirit in this text has taken the place held by the fire of the altar in the ancient sacrifices, and this is a very inspiring thought for our spiritual life. What was the function of the fire in the ancient worship? The problem of the worship in the Old Testament, we could say, was a problem of ascension, that is, how could one make an offering reach all the way to God? The means adopted was the fire of the altar. Through the fire, the victims were transformed into smoke that rose to heaven, all the way to God; God breathed the smoke of the sacrifices that had a pleasant odour; this was the image adopted (cf. *Gn* 8:20-21). However, the Bible makes an important determination on the subject. It specifies that not just any fire could serve this aim. In order that an offering could truly rise all the way to God, a fire that descended from God would be necessary. Only a fire that had descended from God would also be able to rise to heaven, carrying with it the offered victim. The fourth Gospel has a phrase that carries this meaning: "No one has ascended into heaven but he who descended from heaven" (*Jn* 3:13). The Book of Leviticus tells us that the sacrificial worship of the people of God was offered by means of a fire that came from God. At the inauguration of priestly worship, Leviticus says that, "fire came forth from before the LORD and consumed the burnt offering and the fat upon the altar" (*Lv* 9:24). An analogous event can be recalled on the occasion of Solomon's dedication of the Temple. We read in the Second Book of Chronicles: "When Solomon had finished his prayer, fire came down from heaven and consumed the burnt offering and the sacrifices" (*2 Ch* 7:1). In this way, he was assured of the validity of his sacrifices. The Bible prescribes the conserving of the fire that had come from heaven. Leviticus says: "The fire on the altar shall be kept burning on it, it shall not go out" (*Lv* 6:12). So it was always the same fire that had come from heaven that was kept for the sacrificial offerings.

Here we find a profound intuition regarding the nature of sacrifice: to sacrifice is not an action that is accessible to man. It is not a human action. To sacrifice is a divine action. Only God can make an offering sacred. Earthly means are insufficient to

offer a sacrifice; not even the fire is ignited by a man; a heavenly means is needed, indeed, a fire that comes from God himself. Man is not able to sacrifice; he is not able to make sacred; he can only present an offering. God alone can render something sacred by placing it within his divine fire, that is, within his holiness, which is "a devouring fire" (*Dt* 4:24; 9:3).

This intuition is very valid and we must regain it. However, for the Israelites, it was imperfect because the divine fire was still understood in a material way, like the lightning that falls from heaven. The author of the Letter to the Hebrews overcomes this imperfect understanding and, by reflecting on the passion of Jesus, aimed for the true meaning of the symbol. The fire of God is not lightning which falls from the clouds; it is the Spirit of sanctification. The Holy Spirit is alone capable of effecting the true sacrificial transformation, that is, of bringing the sacrifice into the sphere of divine holiness. No material power, not even fire, is truly capable of making an offering rise to God because we are not dealing here with a journey through space; we are concerned with an interior transformation. To approach God, man does not have need of an external movement but a transformation of the heart. Only the Holy Spirit makes such a transformation possible and effective. The sacrifice of Christ did not happen by means of a fire that burned continuously upon the altar of the Temple, but by means of the eternal Spirit who filled the human heart of Christ with an extraordinary strength of love. This is the secret of the internal dynamism of his offering.

Because he was animated by the strength of the Holy Spirit, Jesus had the interior impulse necessary for transforming a death by condemnation into a perfect offering of himself to God on behalf of all. This spiritual strength brought about the true sacrificial transformation. It brought Christ's human nature from the earthly level, that is, from the level of the blood and flesh in which he found himself in virtue of his Incarnation, to the level of the definitive union of God in glory. Jesus passed from this world to the Father, not by means of a spatial journey, but with a transformation, a sanctification as the fourth Gospel tells us: "For their sake, I consecrate myself, that they also may be consecrated in truth" (*Jn* 17:19). It could be translated: For them "I sacrifice" myself. Therefore, to sanctify and to sacrifice are equivalent terms. It is important that we grasp this idea of sacrifice and of offering. It is a positive conception of sanctification by means of the Holy Spirit who pours divine love into our hearts.

Instead of lingering on the aspect of privation or pain, we must turn our attention once again to the aspect of transformation. If the Lord requests an offering of us, it is not to enrich himself for he has no need of our offerings; he had already declared that in the Old Testament; if he asks for an offering, it is in order to communicate his holiness, so as to transform and elevate us by filling us with his Spirit of love. We must understand that, with our own strength, we are incapable of offering a true sacrifice. We can only present our offering and ask the Lord to transform it profoundly by the power of the Holy Spirit.

How can we obtain such strength? We can obtain it just as Jesus obtained it. We see this in chapter 5 which we have already meditated on: "In the days of his flesh, Jesus offered up prayers and supplications, with loud cries and tears, to him who was able to save him from death". Jesus was found "in the days of his flesh", and not in a situation that was already fully spiritual. The oblation did not have an easy point of departure but one that was humble and poor. Christ had assumed our flesh, that is, our fragile, weak and mortal human nature. For this reason, he found himself in a tremendously anxious situation. Starting from such a situation and after praying intensely, Jesus received, in his human nature, a new fullness of the Holy Spirit who gave to him the strength to offer himself with a perfect love.

To obtain the Holy Spirit who transforms our offerings, it is crucial that we follow Christ's example and pray with intensity. Ultimately, every prayer has this aim: to obtain from the Holy

HS via intense Prayer

Spirit so as to open our human nature to the transforming action of God's Holy Spirit who is the Spirit of love. Christ, through intense prayer, inhaled the Holy Spirit, that is, he made him enter into his own blood and in this way, has obtained this strength of love. The Gospel of John gives us an analogous teaching when it says that from the pierced side of Jesus, "there came out blood and water" (*Jn* 19:34), which demonstrated that by means of the passion, the water of the Spirit (cf. *Jn* 7:37-39) was united to the blood of Jesus.

The author of the Letter to the Hebrews says, "the blood of Christ… [shall] purify your conscience from dead works" (*Hb* 9:14) because it is "permeated" by the Holy Spirit through intense prayer. The blood of Christ also opens for us the water of the Spirit, which has a double efficacy: the capacity to purify us from sins and to perfectly serve God.

Therefore, continues the author, he is the Mediator of a New Covenant (*Hb* 9:15). Instead, he has removed the obstacles and has assured our union with God and among ourselves. Just as we breathe the air of the atmosphere so as to oxygenate our blood and to make it capable of vivifying our whole body, so too, we can say that Christ, in his passion, by means of intense prayer, has breathed the Holy Spirit and, in this way, the Holy Spirit has entered into him and has impelled him to offer his own life as a gift of perfect love. *Careful – earning HS?*

Let us then contemplate this mystery with much gratitude because it is an extraordinary gift of God and a model for us. Christ has breathed the Holy Spirit through his intense prayer; likewise, we too must breathe the Holy Spirit with an intense prayer and so become capable of a perfect offering.

13
Efficacy of Christ's oblation
(Hb 10:1-18)

Having considered the offering with which Christ established the New Covenant, let us now reflect on its extraordinary efficacy for the transformation of our life and of the whole world.

Our Western society is characterized by the search for efficiency. This has stimulated innumerable scientists and researchers, urging them to make discoveries that have transformed our conditions of life; however, we must reflect on the progress obtained. We can note straightaway that efficiency depends little on the carrying out of much activity, and still less on the material means at hand; it depends on the level or dimension in which we obtain contact with reality. One who remains at a superficial level will be able to multiply his efforts and his adopted means but new obstacles and difficulties will always put him out. He will not progress much. Instead, one who penetrates the interior of reality through knowledge and by adequate means will be able to obtain much better results with more simple instruments. Let us consider, for example, the perplexity and encumbrance of the old telegraphic systems compared with the simplicity and convenience of the modern *transistor* which is much more powerful. Again, let us consider atomic physics that has sought to penetrate the smallest particles of matter and has obtained extraordinary results both in a positive sense but also, unfortunately, in a negative sense. This depends on the level at which contact with reality is attained. What happens with material reality also happens with spiritual and apostolic realities. What is also important here is not to be agitated and anxious about multiplying one's efforts and means but to go deeper and to attain the heart of reality.

In the Letter to the Hebrews, this kind of efficacy is revealed in the mystery of Christ. The author speaks of it in chapter 10 in which he presents Christ's sacrifice as the decisive intervention that has radically changed the religious situation of all of us. He contraposes it to the multiplicity of the old sacrifices, which remained at a superficial level and were inefficacious.

He begins in this way:

> For, since the law has but a shadow of the good things to come instead of the true form of these realities, it can never, by the same sacrifices which are continuously offered year after year, make perfect those who draw near (Hb 10:1).

Every year they offered sacrifices of expiation but because they remained external, they did not have the hoped for efficacy. The Law did not touch the heart of reality. It remained bound to the shadow of the good things to come. The author explains: "Otherwise, would they not have ceased to be offered? If the worshippers had once been cleansed, they would no longer have had any consciousness of sin" (Hb 10:2). Once the outcome has been achieved, efforts to obtain it cease.

The author continues, "But in these sacrifices, there is a reminder of sin year after year" (Hb 10:3). The unique efficacy of the ancient sacrifices was that of reminding people that they were sinners in need of expiation. However, such expiation was only achieved by external means. It did not have the positive effect of mediation or of purification: "For it is impossible that the blood of bulls and goats should take away sins" (Hb 10:4). It is very clear: the blood of slain animals cannot effect the purification of man's conscience. It was a tentative and completely inefficacious mediation.

For this reason, already in the Old Testament, we find

passages in which God rejects the immolation of animals and the whole ancient ritual system. In Psalm 49, for example, God asks ironically, "Do I eat the flesh of bulls, or drink the blood of goats?" (*Ps* 49/50:13). In the Book of Isaiah: "'What to me is the multitude of your sacrifices?', says the Lord; 'I have had enough of burnt offerings of rams and the fat of fed beasts; I do not delight in the blood of bulls or of lambs, or of he goats'" (*Is* 1:11). The author of the Letter to the Hebrews chooses one of these texts, which has a twofold advantage: that of rejecting every kind of ritual sacrifice and that of proposing an efficacious solution. In Psalm 39/40, the prayer says to God, "Burnt offering and sin offering thou hast not required. Then I said, 'Lo, I come; in the scroll of the Book it is written of me; I delight to do your will'" (*Ps* 39.40:7-9 *LXX*). The author quotes this Psalm which contraposes external sacrifices of whatever kind: holocausts, sacrifices for sin, oblations – this last was a personal offering which consisted in demonstrating that one was disposed to the will of God. It is considered to be a prophetic psalm. It is applied above all to Christ who is the only person capable of perfectly fulfilling the will of God, that is, with perfect love. He is the only one capable of completely bringing about God's plan. Therefore, the author does not hesitate to apply it to Christ and to declare that "Upon entering into the world", Christ has fulfilled this Psalm in himself:

> When he said above, "Thou hast neither desired nor taken pleasure in sacrifices and offerings and burnt offerings and sin offerings" (these are offered according to the law), then he added, "Lo, I have come to do thy will." He abolishes the first in order to establish the second (*Hb* 10:8-9).

He abolishes the old system, which is inefficacious and in its place puts his own perfect offering. Effectively, the ancient system has been eliminated. In the year AD 70, the Temple was destroyed and from then on, the Hebrews no longer had sacrificial worship.

In this magnificent passage, we can admire Christ's love for the Father. It is a love that is expressed as a perfect availability for his will. God has not found worship that was worthy of him on earth; he could not appreciate the sacrifice of animals since it was not possible that the blood of slaughtered animals could enter into communion with God and purify man's conscience. Christ, therefore, after having seen this sad situation, decides to offer to the Father a perfect worship. The profound desire of his heart is that the Father be glorified as he deserves and that his will be done. Jesus does not keep searching for an adequate external offering; he does not ask others to remedy this deficient situation. Instead, he offers himself: "Lo, I have come to do thy will, O God". In place of external material sacrifices, he offers himself. It is his own perfect obedience to the Father as he himself often says in the Gospels. His first spoken word in the Gospel of Luke is his response to his mother when he was twelve years old: "Did you not know that I must be in my Father's house?" (*Lk* 2:49). He has come to truly consecrate himself to the Father's service. It says in the Gospel of John: "For I have come down from heaven, not to do my own will, but the will of him who sent me" (*Jn* 6:38). In his agony, he says, "Father, if thou art willing, remove this cup from me; nevertheless, not my will, but thine be done" (*Lk* 22:42). Note that this is not a prayer of mere resignation as is often thought. It is a powerful expression of love. Jesus knows the will of God. He knows what is best. God's will is for victory over evil by means of the cross. Jesus accepts this will, not with simple resignation but with an impulse of filial love.

The author then speaks of the efficacy of this offering of Jesus, saying that: "By that will, we have been sanctified through the offering of the body of Jesus Christ once and for all" (*Hb* 10:10). Jesus' oblation has changed our whole existence. It has freed us from every obstacle along our way toward God and it has sanctified us. In this way, he has made true worship possible. The perfect communion of man and God is achieved in the glorious body of Christ. We must then maintain this strong conviction: it is not the multiplicity of external activities, personal initiatives and skills that give efficacy to our spiritual and apostolic life; rather it is our personal adhesion to the will of Christ. This adhesion must be internal, that is, of the heart, and must be extended in a coherent way to our whole existence. It must be a vision in favour of love and in view of love. We must hunger and thirst for the will of God as Jesus did of which he states in the Gospel: "My will is to do the will of him who sent me, and to accomplish his work" (*Jn* 4:34). Jesus hungered for the will of God. However, we often ignore this will; we don't want to know it because we fear that it may contrast with our personal projects and will not correspond to our vision. But this is a completely mistaken attachment. In such a case, we would not be well enough aware that the will of God is an expression of his own personal love for each one of us and that it is for us the most precious treasure and the most important means for the efficacy of our actions. In effect, even the simplest action done with love according to the will of God has much greater efficacy than many grandiose actions done according to human ideas. A life lived quietly and according to the will of God, like that of the Virgin Mary, has more value than a series of truly extraordinary exploits achieved by human ambition.

The author now continues to contrapose the ancient sacrifices and the offering of Christ. The ancient sacrifices were continually repeated. Christ's oblation was single and unique. They were continually repeated because they were inefficacious. Christ's oblation is unique because it is perfectly efficacious.

> And every priest stands daily at his service, offering repeatedly the same sacrifices, which can never take away sins. But when Christ had offered for all time a single sacrifice for sins, he sat down at the right hand of God, then to wait until his enemies should be made a stool for his feet. For by a single offering, he has perfected for all time those who are sanctified (*Hb* 10:11-14).

The multiplicity of ancient sacrifices could be interpreted in various ways. For the Hebrew historian, Flavius Josephus, it had a very positive meaning. He recorded with pride the great number of sheep and lambs that on the occasion of the Pasch were immolated at Jerusalem for all the pilgrims. The author of the Letter to the Hebrews, however, examines the situation with greater lucidity. He perceives a sign of failure and inefficacy in the apparent abundance. For him, the sacrifices have been multiplied precisely because their aim has never been achieved. Therefore, the action must be performed again and again. The levitical priests were constantly busy fulfilling so many sacrifices that could never eliminate sins. Christ, instead, is now seated at the right-hand of God and has no need to offer sacrifices, "For by a single offering, he has perfected for all time those who are sanctified" (*Hb* 10:14). With a single offering, Christ has achieved the aim that the old priesthood struggled to achieve without success.

Concerning the efficacy of Christ's sacrifice, the author not only speaks here only of purification and forgiveness as being primary; he also expresses the concept of "making perfect". The Greek word is «τελείων». In the Pentateuch, this word was adopted exclusively for speaking of the consecration of the High Priest. In Hebrew, one uses a slightly strange expression to express the idea of this consecration, namely: *mille yad*, or literally "to fill the hands". When a High Priest was consecrated, his hands were filled. The expression derives from the fact that during the inaugurating ceremony of the sacrificial ministry, the priest received in his hands a part of the victim to be brought to the altar, and so his "hands were filled". The Greek translators of the Septuagint did not want to translate this expression literally; presumably they considered it too material, so instead they used the verb «τελείων»: "to make perfect". In this way, they made the expression more suitable for religious acceptance. The High Priest was called, "He who has been made perfect", «τετελειωμένος» (*Lv* 21:10; *Cf. Hb* 7:28).

The author of the Letter to the Hebrews believes that it is right to speak of perfection with regard to priestly consecration because the priest must be made perfect if he is to enter into relationship with God. However, the author observes that the consecration of the ancient High Priest did not correspond to this law; it did not make him perfect because it consisted in external rites which could transform no one interiorly (cf. *Hb* 7:11;19;28). Christ, however, was truly "made perfect", not by means of inefficacious external rites but by means of existential sufferings that were offered with love (cf. *Hb* 2:10; 5:8-9). Furthermore, the unique offering of Christ had a double effect, that is, it had a twofold efficacy, namely: it conferred perfection on Christ and it conferred perfection on us (*Hb* 5:9; 10:14). In his passion and resurrection, Christ was at the same time both active and passive. He received perfection and he communicated it to us – and this perfection is a priestly perfection. As I explained, it is a perfection of the relationship of filial docility to God and fraternal compassion with us.

The statement: "By a single offering, he has perfected for all time those who are sanctified", contains something surprising. On the one hand, it indicates something that has already been achieved. Christ *has made* perfect, «ετελειώσεν». The Greek verb indicates a reality that has already been communicated. On the other hand, the phrase continues to indicate a reality that is becoming, that is, a dynamism: he has made perfect those whom he is sanctifying, «τους 'αγιαζομενως», that is, those who have now received the sanctification, albeit progressively. It is a work in progress. These are the two aspects of our religious situation that result from Christ's oblation. On the part of Christ, all has now been achieved: he has made us perfect. On our part, all is in a process of realization. Our sanctification continues to be achieved little by little. The author has had the audacity to place these two statements together although they seem to be contrasting. However, they really do correspond to our Christian situation. In this regard, theologians speak of an "already accomplished" and of a "not yet".

We find ourselves in a situation that is both dynamic and serenely tranquil. On the one hand, Christ awakens in us a dynamic love that requires our continued effort. On the other hand, he has already given us security and peace. "Peace I leave with you; my peace I give to you; not as the world gives do I give to you" (*Jn* 14:27). The victory has already been won (cf. *Jn* 16:33). However, we still need to struggle faithfully and generously so as to receive this victory in our spiritual life and apostolate. There is nothing lacking in Christ's oblation. Only we are lacking in our application of this completely and perfectly efficacious mystery. Therefore, we must march onwards with a sure commitment to success because the love of Christ has been dynamically and serenely given to us.

14
Privileges and requirements of the union with our High Priest (Hb 10:19-25)

After having exposed his doctrine on the priesthood and sacrifice of Christ, the author of the Letter to the Hebrews draws consequences for the Christian people, that is, for us. He describes our situation after the death and resurrection of Christ. It is the situation of the New Covenant, which is a privileged and marvellous situation. Then he indicates the expected and corresponding attitudes. He does this in a passage of chapter 10 starting from verse 19. It is a very important passage. Perhaps it is even the heart of the whole Letter because it once again takes up the doctrine and proposes a program of Christian life. It includes two closely connected parts that are also clearly distinct. The first part is descriptive; the second is exhortative. The first part shows that we possess three things: a right of entrance into the Sanctuary; a way to walk so as to reach this Sanctuary; and a guide who leads us on the way. The second part invites us to assume three attitudes: that of faith, hope, and charity. The descriptive part comes first because it is the basis of the exhortation. Exegetes note that in the Bible the indicative always precedes the imperative. The indicative presents the wonderful gifts of God; the imperative exhorts that these gifts be actively received and not be allowed to slip by. The New Covenant is above all a gift that God has made and continues to make. We must, therefore, receive this gift, committing ourselves to it and making it operative in our life.

The author does not use the term "Covenant" here. However, the reality he describes corresponds perfectly to the Covenant situation because it concerns a situation characterized by an absence of separations and by the ease of communication. Let us read the text, the first part of which is descriptive and the second, starting with "Let us…" is exhortative:

> Therefore, brethren, since we have confidence to enter the sanctuary by the blood of Jesus, by the new and living way which he opened for us through the curtain, that is, through his flesh, and since we have a great priest over the house of God, let us draw near with a true heart in full assurance of faith, with our hearts sprinkled clean from an evil conscience and our bodies washed with pure water. Let us hold fast the confession of our hope without wavering, for he who promised is faithful; and let us consider how to stir up one another to love and good works, not neglecting to meet together, as is the habit of some, but encouraging one another, and all the more as you see the Day drawing near (*Hb* 10:19-25).

At the beginning of this text, the author uses the term "brethren" which expresses the union of believers in the New Covenant. They are not only brothers *of* Christ; they are also brothers *in* Christ (cf. *Hb* 2:11-12). At the end, he returns to insist on this fraternal union, exhorting all to charity. In this small passage, however, he insists above all on the relationship of believers with God. In the Old Covenant, this relationship was obstructed in various ways. In the New Covenant, all believers have "the full right" of entrance into the Sanctuary so as to draw near to God.

The translations often have "confidence" in place of "right", but the Greek term «παρρησίαν» (*parresia*)[6]* contains more than

---

6 Translator's note: In a meeting with the author during the *Year of the Priest* (2009-2010), I learned that this greek term was the Cardinal's inspiration for the choice of the title for the Spiritual Exercises.

just the subjective disposition of 'confidence'; it also indicates an objective right, that is, the freedom to come and express oneself. The *parresia* was characteristic of the Greek city; at Athens or in other democratic cities of Greece, the citizens enjoyed the *parresia*, that is, the right to intervene and speak in the deliberative assembly so as to express and defend one's position. This right of free speech was not recognized for strangers or for slaves. This term *parresia* is often used in the New Testament to characterize the Christian situation as one of freedom, with the right of free speech and the right of access. The Christian has the freedom of the children of God, that is, he has the full right of entrance into the divine Sanctuary. All the legal separations of the Old Testament have been abolished.

In the Old Covenant, there was the separation between the people and the priests. The people were never authorized to enter into the Temple building; they could only stand in the courts. The priests enjoyed the right of penetrating the inner part of the building but the simple priests were also separated from the High Priests. The first could not enter into the "Most Holy" part but only into the "Holy" part of the edifice. Only the High Priest enjoyed the right of penetrating into the "Most Holy" place, that is, the Holy of Holies, but only once a year. There was also the separation of the priest and the victim. The priest could not offer himself because he was neither worthy nor capable. He must offer an animal as victim although it was not capable of sanctifying him. Lastly, there was the separation between the victim and God. An animal cannot enter into communion with God.

Now, however, through Christ's offering, all believers enjoy the right to enter into the Sanctuary and in this regard, it is no longer the inauthentic Sanctuary fabricated by human hands. Now it is the true Sanctuary, that is, entrance into intimacy with God. This right of entrance is established in the blood of Christ, as the author says literally, because this blood has become the blood of the Covenant, having been poured out as a most generous offering which has abolished all the old separations and has established full communication between the people and God.

With his own offering, Christ has abolished the separation between the victim and God. This is because he was a victim who is always pleasing to God. He is a victim "without blemish" as the author says (9:14). He is a victim who has perfectly and lovingly fulfilled the will of God (cf. 10:9). Therefore, he is able to be pleasing to him. At the same time, Christ has abolished the separation between victim and himself as priest because he has offered himself (9:14): he is the victim. He [God] accepted the priest at the same moment in which he accepted the victim and has elevated him to be near him in glory. Finally, Christ has even abolished the separation between the people and the priest because his own offering was an act of total solidarity with all of us. It was an act in which the priestly consecration conferred on him was at the same time communicated to us (cf. 5:9; 10:14).

In this way, the blood of Christ has truly become "The blood of the Covenant" (cf. 10:29; 13:20). It is a blood that establishes a new situation, which cannot be verified by any preceding event. St Paul affirms in the Letter to the Ephesians that we have full freedom of access to the Father in Christ Jesus our Lord. We have the *parresia,* that is, the "boldness and confidence of access through our faith in him" (*Eph* 3:12). The blood of Jesus possesses an extraordinary power of cohesion; it establishes communion with God and among the brethren. Just as our blood establishes a vital communion among all the cells of our body, in the same way, the blood of Christ establishes communion in the body of Christ of which we are the members.

The author then goes on to express two other aspects of our situation. In order to enter into the Sanctuary, it is not enough to have the right of access. It is also necessary to have a way to follow and a guide that precedes us on that way. We find all this in Christ. In him, we have "the new and living way which he opened for us through the curtain, that is, through his flesh" (*Hb* 10:20). Here, also, we find newly expressed a change of situation with respect to the worship of the Old Testament. Earlier, the author affirmed that in the Old Covenant, the way of the true Sanctuary had not yet been "manifested" (*Hb* 9:8), that is, it was still not known. It was not understood in which direction to go and therefore, it was impossible to have full communication with God. Now, instead, we have the *way* which is the human nature of Jesus transformed in his sacrifice. The author says that Christ himself in his Paschal Mystery has inaugurated this way. In order to enter into heavenly intimacy with God in his human nature, Christ has adopted this *way*, which is precisely his own glorified humanity. This *way* is "new"; it did not previously exist; it is a new creation. He is the *way* by which the New Covenant arrives and it is channelled by him who has received the new heart and the new spirit, that is, the Spirit of God.

In saying "new", the author adopts a rare Greek term «πρόσφατος» which we find in Greek translations of the Book of Ecclesiastes (Qoheleth). Disconsolate, Qoheleth said: "There is nothing new under the sun" (*Ec* 1:9). We are in a cyclic world; it is always the same old things returning which often give the impression of newness but in reality are not new. This statement of Qoheleth is no longer true and we can no longer accept it. There *is* a newness, there is a wonderful newness; we are no longer enclosed in a cyclic world in which the same old things can keep returning. We are in the new perspective that is opened by Christ's resurrection.

It is a "living way", since it concerns the risen Christ, that is, "the living" (Lk 24:5) *par excellence*. "Christ being raised from the dead will never die again. Death no longer has dominion over him", says St Paul (*Rm* 6:9). The new and living *way* is Christ himself. To speak of a new and living way is another way to designate "the greater and more perfect Tent" (*Hb* 9:11) through which Christ himself has entered into the divine Sanctuary. It concerns the glorified humanity of Jesus, which has become for us the unique way of access to God.

We must come to appreciate the extraordinary newness introduced into the world by Christ's resurrection. It gives us the capacity "to be transformed by the renewal of our mind" as St Paul says (*Rm* 12:2) and "to put on the new nature" (*Ep* 4:24). We are not called to live in the old world, but in the new creation, with a new heart and a new spirit. The search for the will of God introduces us to the newness because as I have already said, in the New Testament, this will is not a fixed code but an on-going creation. In this regard, it gives me pleasure to cite a poem of my confrere who died a few years ago, Fr Rimaud, who put it in this way: "*Invente avec ton Dieu l'avenir qu'il te donne, invente avec ton Dieu tout un monde plus beau*". "Make with your God the future that he gives you. With your God, make the whole world more beautiful". It seems to me that this truly expresses the orientation of the Christian life and in particular the orientation of the apostolic life. We must always find Christian newness, which is like an inexhaustible spring continually created by God.

The third notation speaks to us of the guide on this way. We have "a great priest over the house of God" (*Hb* 10:21). Here, the author gives a hint of the first quality of a priest which is to be worthy of faith and, therefore, authoritative. The expression that he adopts here is the same expression found in chapter 3 concerning Christ the High Priest who is worthy of faith. There, the author had said: "Christ was faithful over God's house as a son". We are his house. Therefore, we have a priest who guides us toward God so as to present us to him. The New Covenant is not like the Old. It is not an impersonal institution, a law written on stone. The New Covenant is a person, a living reality. It is Christ risen. The New Covenant exists for the person of the risen Christ and in the person of the risen Christ.

So this is our situation and it is a truly privileged one. We have the right to enter the Sanctuary; we have the way; we have the guide; we are lacking nothing.   Having all this, we are invited to proceed with promptness. The author returns to this invitation at the beginning of the exhortative part: "Let us therefore approach with a sincere heart". Here also, we can note a strong contrast with the old prohibition against approaching the Sanctuary. In the Old Testament, it was strictly prohibited to the faithful to "come near", that is, to enter into the edifice of the Temple. If anyone did so, he would deserve the death penalty. In the Book of Numbers, it says many times that he who comes near will be punished by death: "No one will approach if he is not a descendant of Aaron. If anyone else comes near, he is to be put to death" (*Nb* 1:51; 3:10; 38).

As we have already seen, the High Priest could only enter once a year into the Most Holy part of the Temple, and only for the purpose of observing a whole series of minutely prescribed rites. Now, instead, we are all invited to come near to God, to enter into intimate contact with him. We have good reasons for thinking that the author made this exhortation during a Eucharistic celebration, perhaps even during several Eucharistic celebrations because, as I have already said, he was a travelling apostle; we see that at the end. It seems to me very probable that he composed this magnificent homily in order to preach it in Christian assemblies that involved the celebration of the Eucharist. This phrase corresponds perfectly to the Eucharistic dynamism in every way. The author speaks here of the blood of Christ, the flesh of Christ, (just like in Jesus' discourse on the bread of life) and the person of Christ the Priest. He says that these three realities are now available to us. Where are they available? They are available in the Eucharistic celebration.

In defining the fundamental orientations of the life of the New Covenant, the author does not name the moral virtues; he does not make a moral exhortation; rather, he makes a theological exhortation. Sometimes Christian preachers make too many moral exhortations and not enough theological exhortations, which are more important. The author names the three theological virtues: faith, hope and charity. He could have named the moral or cardinal virtues, but he did not because these virtues do not have a direct relationship with the New Covenant. Instead, the theological virtues are essential for the life of the New Covenant as they concern the relationship with God and relationships with the brethren. In this passage, the author actually anticipates the entire remainder of his homily. In chapter 11, he will speak of faith; in chapter 12 he will speak of hope and its special endurance; and in the last part of his homily, he will speak of the relationship with God and charity among the brethren.

The Old Testament had already insisted strongly on faith and confidence but it was a major source of complaint because the people did not correspond to this requirement. On the other hand, in the course of Israel's history, the theological perspective was obscured by ever-stronger preoccupations with observance. The Hebrews were preoccupied, above all, with perfect observance of all the traditions and commandments. Instead, the New Testament does not insist so much on legal observances but exhorts all to have faith, hope and charity.

The first condition that the Letter to the Hebrews repeats for coming near to God is not the fulfillment of the Law but the adhesion of faith to God through Christ's mediation. Here, we find again the Pauline doctrine, which rejects the demands of the Law, and makes the gift of faith the basis of all laws. The nuances however, are different. Paul assumes a juridical perspective. He criticizes the Law because it was not capable of justifying men, all of whom are sinners. The author of the Letter to the Hebrews puts it in a perspective of mediation. He criticizes the Law because it is not capable of instituting an efficacious sacrifice, a valid priesthood or an irrevocable covenant. The invitation to faith is based upon the perfect efficacy of the sacrifice and of Christ's priesthood, which constitutes a perfect mediation. Faith is an attitude of the heart, "For man believes with his heart", says

St Paul (*Rm* 10:10). Our author, however, exhorts, "Let us draw near with a true heart with full assurance of faith". Where are Christians to procure this sincere heart when the Old Testament tells us that all men have a duplicitous, even a treacherous heart? The author explains: "Let us draw near with our hearts sprinkled clean from an evil conscience and our bodies washed with pure water". Commentators see a basis in this phrase for a twofold reference to Baptism, under the aspects of the external rite and of the interior effect.

The author then goes on to speak of hope: "Let us hold fast the confession of our heart without wavering, for he who promised is faithful" (*Hb* 10:23). Throughout the Letter to the Hebrews, hope is inseparable from faith. Even when the author wants to define faith, he defines it firstly in relationship to hope. The Holy Father has recalled this in his second Encyclical. So what is faith? "Now faith is the assurance of things hoped for" (*Hb* 11:1). Faith is, therefore, a way of possessing, in anticipation, the things for which we hope. Hope expresses the dynamic aspect of faith. The message that we receive is not the revelation of an abstract truth to be recorded. It is the revelation of a person who is the *way*, the *truth* and the *life* (*Jn* 14:6). Therefore, our faith produces hope.

In the New Covenant, many precious gifts were already communicated. However, we look forward to a complete fullness. We hope to receive "the promised eternal inheritance" (*Hb* 9:15) and to enter forever into "a heavenly homeland" (11:16), that is, into God's "rest" (*Hb* 4:10-11). From the moment that Christ reached his destiny, our hope is secure, as the author says in chapter 6 (*Hb* 6:18-20).

Finally, the author focuses his exhortation on Christian love, that is, on charity. Literally, he invites us to a "paroxysm of love" (10:24). The relationship between covenant and charity is ever so intimate, because charity always presents two dimensions: union with God in love and union with the brethren in generous service.   These two dimensions are the two dimensions of the New Covenant.   At the end, the author makes a still more pressing exhortation referring to the day: "And all the more, as you see the day drawing near", that is, the day of the Lord of which the prophet spoke and of which Jesus also spoke.   How could they see that the day was approaching?   The most likely hypothesis, it would appear to me, is that the author hints here at the first uprising that was stirred up in Palestine about the year 65/66, which led them to foresee the Jewish War that led to the destruction of Jerusalem and the burning of the Temple. This was the end of the Old Covenant from this point of view. Jesus predicted this day (Cf. *Mt* 24:1-2 and parallel verses) when he said: "This generation will not pass away till all these things take place" (*Mt* 24:34). Then he called everyone to vigilance (*Mt* 24:42). Based on the rapid approach of the day, the author of the Letter to the Hebrews, therefore, draws his motive for exhorting Christians to be more fervent and active in charity.

So the dynamism of the New Covenant is manifested: it is an intense dynamism that leads towards the encounter with the Lord.   The situation of the New Covenant is a privileged situation of communion with God, made possible by Christ.   It is not a passive and pointless situation but one that is active and demanding.

In prayer, let us give thanks to the Lord for having put us in this privileged situation.   Let us offer ourselves to him, so as to respond to his gifts with a great faith, with an indestructible hope and with a generous charity.

15
The Blood of the Covenant and the Resurrection of Christ
(Hb 13:20-21)

I now propose to you a meditation on the solemn conclusion of the homily contained in the Letter to the Hebrews. The author concludes his homily with a solemn wish that speaks of the resurrection. It is a passage composed of two verses (*Hb* 13:20-21). The first takes up again the doctrine espoused by the author and the second recaptures the exhortations and ends with a doxology. The conclusion formula is very beautiful:

> Now may the God of peace who brought again from the dead our Lord Jesus, the great shepherd of the sheep, by the blood of the eternal covenant, equip you with everything good that you may do his will, working in you that which is pleasing in his sight, through Jesus Christ; to whom be glory for ever and ever. Amen.

These two verses again recapture the theme of the Covenant, but in a new light by speaking of an "eternal Covenant" which is the only time this expression is found in the New Testament. The expression, "God of peace" is already clearly related to the Covenant. The Lord revealed himself as the God of peace when, in Christ, he reconciled the world to himself and established the New Covenant, in this way eliminating every kind of separation and division. In the Second Letter to the Corinthians, we read: "All this is from God, who through Christ reconciled us to himself … in Christ, God was reconciling the world to himself, not accounting their trespasses against them, and entrusting to us the message of reconciliation" (*2 Co* 5:18-19). God is truly the God of a very active peace, who propagates reconciliation and union among all.

The decisive intervention of the God of peace is described in new terms: the author speaks for the first time of the resurrection of Christ. In his homily, he referred frequently to Christ's glorification, that is, of his entrance into the heavenly Sanctuary, but he did not speak explicitly of the resurrection. This passage is the only one in which he does so. The author also refers to the resurrection in an original rather than in a traditional way; he adopts a passage of Isaiah for this purpose, which recalls the divine work of salvation during the Exodus. Isaiah writes:

> Then he remembered the days of old, and Moses his servant. Where is he who brought up out of the sea the shepherds of his flock? … Who divided the waters before them to make for himself an everlasting name, who led them through the depths? Like a horse in the desert, they did not stumble … so thou didst lead thy people, to make for thyself a glorious name (*Is* 63:11-14).

Isaiah calls Moses "the shepherd of the flock" [of God]. The Septuagint has translated this "the shepherd of the sheep" and the author of the Letter naturally recalls this expression (Cf. *Jn* 10:11;14) but he underlines the superiority of Jesus with respect to Moses. Moses is simply "the shepherd of the sheep"; Jesus is "the great shepherd", that is, the great High Priest. Peter, in his First Letter, uses a similar expression for Christ. Literally, he calls him the "chief shepherd" («αρχιποίμεν» *1 Pt* 5:4). Of course, the translations change this and use two words but a literal English translation of what Peter says would be "arch-shepherd" which brings to mind the «αρχιερευς» (*archiereus*) which is "High Priest". The superiority of Jesus with respect to Moses is indicated by the fact that while Moses caused the waters of the sea to rise in order to lead the people to a pastured land, that is, the Promised Land, Jesus rose from the dead to introduce us to an eternal inheritance. With the two expressions, the author wishes to point out that the resurrection of Jesus is not only an individual event, that is, Christ is not glorified for himself. It is an event that involves all of us. Christ glorified is the shepherd of the sheep. He opens for all the sheep the way of new life, that is, the life of resurrection. Jesus has risen as "the pioneer of salvation" (*Hb* 2:10), as "the first-born from the dead" (*Col* 1:18) and as "the first fruits" (*1 Co* 15:20) of the new creation; this is the ecclesial aspect of Christ's resurrection.

The expression used by the author can be surprising: he says that God has raised Christ from death, literally: "in the blood of the eternal covenant". The RSV translates it: "by the blood of the eternal covenant". What does this mean? The author attributes to the blood of Christ a decisive function for his resurrection. Why is he able to do so? It is on account of the relationship that he perceives between the blood and the Spirit which was first expressed in the phrase which we meditated on yesterday, where he says, "How much more shall the blood of Christ, who through the eternal spirit offered himself without blemish to God, purify your conscience from dead works" (*Hb* 9:14). This enables us to reflect on the resurrection in a new way.

The first formulations of the Christian faith only highlighted the obvious contrast between the death of Jesus and his resurrection. Men had him put to death; God raised him up and restored him to life (*Cf. Acts* 3:15; 4:10). Consequently, it was understood that the resurrection of Jesus occurred through the Spirit of Life, that is, through the Holy Spirit, as St Paul clearly says at the beginning of the Letter to the Romans (*Rm* 1:4). Ezekiel had already shown that resurrection is a work of the Spirit: in his famous vision of the dry bones, he received orders to call upon the *ruah,* that is, the "breath" or "wind", ultimately, the Spirit, so that he might enter into the bones and cause them to live again (*Ez* 37:9). The Spirit is the breath of God that gives life.

The subsequent deepening of the Christian faith noticed that the action of the Holy Spirit did not begin with the resurrection but had already been manifested during the life of Jesus and, in particular, during his passion. The author of the Letter to the Hebrews helps us to understand this: Jesus prayed constantly to the Father. In response to his prayer, he received from the Father the Spirit who gave him the strength to transform his own death, which was an event of rupture, into an event of communion, in this way, completely overturning the meaning of death. So the death of Jesus has become the foundation of the New Covenant, thanks to the action of the Holy Spirit. The blood of Jesus has been imbued with the Holy Spirit through his intense prayer and his perfect docility to the Father and has become the source of new life, the source of resurrection.

We can deepen a little the relationship between the blood and the Spirit, according to the Old Testament. For the ancient mentality, the blood was sacred because it signified life, which is a gift of God. The Bible teaches us that in the blood, there is the *nefesh* (Hebrew: the vital principle, the breath of life, the soul – not necessarily a rational soul, but a soul insofar as it gives life to the body). In fact, a passage of Deuteronomy says that the blood itself is *nefesh* (*Dt* 12:23): the blood is the vital principle. Modern science has confirmed this intuition with the discovery of the oxygenating function of the blood. Our blood has a very intimate relationship with our "breath". In order to live, we need our "breath" to enter into our blood, that is, the air that we breathe must enter into our blood, enriching it with oxygen, so that the blood can communicate this oxygen to every cell in the body and give it life. Without this oxygen, a cell will die. So there is an essential relationship between the breath and the blood just as between the Spirit and the blood because in Hebrew, the word, *ruah* means breath or spirit.

These elements are taken up in depth by the author of the

Letter to the Hebrews who shows us an intimate relationship between the blood of Christ and the Holy Spirit. In this case, he is less concerned with a biological phenomenon than with a spiritual reality. Since we breathe the air of the atmosphere to oxygenate our blood and make it capable of carrying life to every cell of our body, so Christ in his passion, by means of his intense prayer, has "breathed" the Holy Spirit. In order to overcome the fear of death, he prayed with supplication and received the Holy Spirit who entered into him and inspired him to offer his very life as a gift of love. So we can say that, in the passion, the blood of Christ was imbued with the Holy Spirit and acquired the capacity to communicate new life and to establish the New Covenant. The blood of Christ became, for his human nature, the vital principle that communicated the new life of communion with God and with the brethren. In a certain sense, we can say that the Incarnation of the Son of God, which flows by means of his passion, has involved a "blood transfusion" of the Holy Spirit, that is, the passion, has made the human nature of Christ, and especially his blood, the instrument that communicates the Holy Spirit.

This doctrine is also found in the fourth Gospel. The Gospel of John shows us an intimate relationship between the passion of Jesus and the gift of the Holy Spirit. When Jesus says: "Father, the hour has come; glorify your Son that the Son may glorify thee" (*Jn* 17:1), he is referring to the passion in which the Father glorifies the Son thanks to the abundant gift of the Holy Spirit. Therefore, we see a special relationship between Christ's resurrection and his blood; the blood communicates to us the new life of the risen Christ. It purifies and vivifies us, thanks to its relationship with the Holy Spirit.

The second verse of the passage expresses a hope with regard to our spiritual life: "May the God of peace … equip you with everything good that you may do his will, working in you that which is pleasing in his sight, through Jesus Christ". Here, we can note a new element. After having wished the Christians to be rendered by God capable of fulfilling his will as Christ himself fulfilled the will of the Father in the passion, the author adds, "That which is pleasing in his sight". It seems to me that, in this way, he has indicated the most profound element of the New Covenant, namely: the fact that we receive in ourselves the action of God himself. In the Old Covenant, God prescribed what must be done. He prescribed it through an external law. This kind of covenant did not work because man is not capable of fulfilling God's will by his own strength. Therefore, the Lord willed to institute a New Covenant, promising to write his laws onto man's heart (*Jr* 31:33) and to give him a new heart, that is, to give him his Holy Spirit (*Ez* 36:26-27). This means that in the New Covenant, he who acts is God himself and we must receive his action in us. Our Christian acting is the hidden acting of God in us with faith and gratitude through Jesus Christ, the Mediator of the New Covenant.

This doctrine of the Letter to the Hebrews is not isolated in the New Testament. St Paul also declares to the Philippians, "God is at work in you, both to will and to work for his good pleasure" (*Ph* 2:13). God is involved in the achievement of our action. This statement of Paul corresponds to the promise given by God through the lips of Ezekiel, namely, that he would put his Spirit into our hearts so as to make us capable of observing all his decrees. "I will do that you may do", God literally says in the prophecy of Ezekiel (*Ez* 36:27). God himself acts that we may act, therefore, the New Covenant not only consists in receiving the Laws of God interiorly, but in receiving the action of God himself in us. We find a very profound teaching on this point in the fourth Gospel. It concerns the works of Christ as a gift of the Father. Jesus says twice that the works that he performs are a gift of the Father. He literally says: "For the works which the Father has granted me to accomplish, these very works ... bear me witness that the Father has sent me" (*Jn* 5:36). In the priestly prayer: "Having accomplished the work which thou gavest me to do" (*Jn* 17:4). The exact meaning of the Greek here cannot have the idea of the Father merely designating a "job" to the Son, as some less than careful translations imply. Rather, God the Father has entrusted divine works to Christ. "The Son can do nothing of his own accord, but only what he sees the Father doing; for whatever he does, that the Son does likewise" (*Jn* 5:19).

Just as Jesus received his works from the Father, so also we must receive our works from Jesus. He must not only live in us, he must also act in us and with us. We are united to him like branches to the vine; after all, it is the vine that produces the activity of the branches. "As the branch cannot bear fruit by itself, unless it abides in the vine, neither can you, unless you abide in me. I am the vine, you are the branches" (*Jn* 15:4-5).

Jesus also says a surprising thing in this regard in his discourse after the Last Supper: "Truly, truly, I say to you, he who believes in me will also do the works that I do; and greater works than these will he do, because I go to the Father" (*Jn* 14:12). Here, the various translations put a fullstop: Jesus goes to the Father. The disciples are therefore free to do their works that are greater than those of Jesus. It is an enormous error of punctuation. It is necessary to read the whole passage to understand it correctly: the believer "Will do greater things, because I go to the Father *and whatever you ask in my name, I will do it,* in order that the Father may be glorified in the Son" (*Jn* 14:12-13). The disciples will do greater works than those of Jesus during their earthly life because Jesus, now that he has been glorified, will *himself* be able to do these greater works; he will do them and the disciples will do them with him. St Paul did greater things than Jesus; Jesus, however, limited his ministry to Palestine while Paul extended his apostolate to many countries. However, Paul received his works from Christ; he was aware of not being the principal actor; the principal actor was Christ, who "worked through [his apostle]" (*Cf. Rm* 15:18-19). We also must make ourselves available to Christ so as to do his great works *with him*. We must ask the Father to achieve in us, through Christ, what is pleasing to him and, in this way, make ourselves instruments for his work of salvation in the world.

16
Union with Christ and baptismal priesthood (1 Pt 2:4-5)

As we have seen, the Letter to the Hebrews strongly emphasizes the radical newness of the sacrifice and the priesthood of Christ. One aspect of this newness is the openness to participation. The ancient priesthood was not open to anyone for participation. It was founded on a system of sanctification that was characterized by separation. Therefore, it was exclusively reserved to the priests and to the High Priest. When the High Priest entered into the Holy of Holies, no one else could follow or accompany him. The Book of Leviticus determines: "There shall be no man in the tent of meeting" (*Lv* 16:17), that is, no one, in the first part called the "holy place". Instead, the priesthood of Christ is fully opened to participation, because it has been founded on an act of complete fraternal solidarity with us sinners. The Letter to the Hebrews affirms that by his oblation, Christ "has made perfect those who are sanctified" (*Hb* 10:14) and we have seen that "to make perfect" also means, in the context, "to consecrate as priest". With his oblation, Christ has consecrated as priests those who are sanctified. All Christians now enjoy priestly privileges that are even better privileges than those of the ancient High Priest himself, because they have the full right of entrance into the true Sanctuary without any limit of time. Furthermore, they are invited to offer their sacrifices continually to God through Christ; the author tells us in chapter 13 that the sacrifice, which is a eucharist, that is, a "sacrifice of praise", is a life of charity (*Hb* 13:15-16).

On the other hand, the author also shows that the leaders of the Church, whom he calls «'ηγουμένοι» (*hegoumenoi*) have a special participation in the priesthood of Christ, in the sense of the authority to communicate the Word of God (*Hb* 13:7) in union with Christ the High Priest who is worthy of faith for dealings with God. Furthermore, they enjoy this participation in the sense of the priestly mercy of Christ that leads them to watch over the good of souls (*Hb* 13:17). However, the author of the Letter to the Hebrews applies the title of priest neither to the Christians nor to their leaders.

Instead, St Peter, in his First Letter, applies to all the community of believers, a priestly title which he calls «ιεράτευμα» (*hierateuma*) (*1 Pt* 2:5, 9), a term that means, "priestly nature". It is a collective term that is found in the Greek translation of the Old Testament (*Ex* 19:6 *LXX*). St Peter, in this splendid passage of chapter 2, expresses the whole dynamism of the new life of the believers, the fruit of the passion and the resurrection of Christ. This passage is of capital importance for our spiritual and ecclesial life. Peter begins by demonstrating the conditions of ecclesial life. He is speaking to some newly-baptized, whom he compares to the newborn: "So put away all malice and all guile and insincerity and envy and all slander. Like newborn babes, long for the pure spiritual milk, that by it you may grow up to salvation; for you have tasted the kindness of the Lord" (*1 Pt* 2:1-3). Then comes the second part: "Come to him, that living stone, rejected by men but in God's sight chosen and precious; and like living stones be yourselves built into a spiritual house, to be a holy priesthood, to offer spiritual sacrifices acceptable to God through Jesus Christ" (*1 Pt* 2:4-5).

In this phrase, the relationship with the Lord is powerfully expressed. Peter says that we must hold firm to the Lord; Christian conversion is always conversion to Christ and through Christ to God. This conversion also assumes a communitarian and an ecclesial dimension. When we enter into contact with Christ, we are assimilated to him and we are integrated into a spiritual house that is founded on him who is a Sanctuary of God. In this way, we are wrested from the dispersion of our individualism and are all reunited together to form the house of God. This involves a very strong union because we are not just near one another as if we were all inside a building. We could already appreciate such a relationship. In this case, we are bonded together like the stones that form the edifice. When people gather together indoors, for a time, they can still leave. They can go outside and disperse when they are ready. However, the stones that form an edifice are bonded together in a definitive way. They can only be torn apart by a violence which damages the whole edifice. What we have here is an ideal of very strong unity. It ought to give great joy but it is also very demanding.

This analogy of construction is certainly not new; it was adopted by the Scriptures and by Jesus himself. St Peter could not have had a more vivid idea since he had received his new name "Peter" on Jesus' initiative precisely in relation to the construction of the Church. Jesus had said to him: "You are *Kefa* - that is, rock – and on this rock I will build my Church" (*Mt* 16:18; *Cf. Jn* 1:42). Here, St Peter designates Christ himself as the "Living stone, rejected by men but in God's sight, chosen and precious" (*1 Pt* 2:4). Nearly all the words of this rather long expression come from the prophetic texts that the Apostle then cites in the subsequent verses; only the qualifying adjective "living" is new. What does the Apostle want to say? Does he perhaps want to emphasize that the metaphor suggests the solidity of rock but not its inertia? This is not the reason. Peter is hinting at the Paschal Mystery. Christ, by means of his resurrection, has become "the living stone". He has manifested himself as the living. St Luke, or more specifically, the angels in his Gospel ask: "Why do you seek the living among the dead?" (*Lk* 24:5). Christ is the living man who has decisively triumphed over all the powers of death.

St Peter invites us to come near to the risen Christ in his Paschal Mystery and to fully adhere to him in faith.

However, the Paschal Mystery embraces two inseparable aspects. St Peter also took care to record the other aspect. Jesus has been rejected by men in his passion, and then glorified by God in his resurrection. Note that Peter does not polemicize against the Jews, he does not say "rejected by the Jews", but "rejected by men". We all share responsibility for the passion of Jesus; we must not put the blame solely on the Jews. Men rejected Jesus; they considered him a stone to be rejected, to be cast out with the rejected as it is written in Psalm 117/118, which Jesus himself quoted after the parable of the murderous vineyard tenants: "The very stone which the builders rejected has become the head of the corner" (*v.* 22; *Mt* 21:42). God has gone and selected again this stone that had been thrown away among the rejected. He has chosen it and has reaffirmed its supreme value for the construction of the edifice. Raised from the dead, Christ has become the foundation of a new construction. He is the living stone to which innumerable other stones will be added.

See how St Peter expresses the ecclesial aspect of the Paschal Mystery, which we also found in the Letter to the Hebrews. St Peter is inspired by the Psalm that speaks of the cornerstone, namely: that which gives the edifice its solidity. Peter gives us to understand that Christ's resurrection is not a glorification that is relevant only to the individual: on the contrary, Christ's resurrection constitutes him the cornerstone of a new edifice which is the centre and source of unity. Christ has died and has been raised "to gather into one the children of God who are scattered abroad" (*Jn* 11:52). Those who approach him in fullness of faith are transformed by contact with him. They also become living stones, because the resurrected life pervades and transforms them. God regenerates them through Jesus' resurrection, as St Peter says at the beginning of his Letter (*1 Pt* 1:3), and are incorporated into the new edifice. We must understand the resurrection in this way and adhere to the risen Jesus so as to be pervaded by his life and profoundly transformed.

This new edifice is literally called "a spiritual house". How can we understand this expression? We can firstly interpret it in a general way, saying that Christians are not called to construct a material house but a spiritual edifice. This interpretation is not false but it is insufficient. The expression has a stronger meaning. Here, "house" means "house of God", that is, "a Temple". In the Old Testament, in fact, the Hebrew word *beth* or "house" was often adopted without further determination to mean "the Temple of Jerusalem". Here, St Peter does not have in mind any edifice other than a Temple, that is, a Sanctuary. We see this immediately after because he speaks of priesthood and of an offering pleasing to God. So it concerns a new Temple that substitutes the Temple of Jerusalem.

Here it is a case of recalling once again the history of the construction, destruction and reconstruction of the Temple of Jerusalem. The point of departure, as you know so well, is the oracle of the prophet Nathan, in the Second Book of Samuel (*2 S* 7). The idea had come to David of constructing a beautiful house for God. The ark of God was still in a tent and he considered this to be insufficient. However, the prophet was sent by God to say: "Would you build me a house to dwell in? The Lord will make you a house ... I will raise up your offspring after you ... and I will establish his kingdom ... he shall build a house for my name" (*2 S* 7:5-13). Nathan's oracle found its first fulfillment in the history of Solomon, David's son and his successor, who constructed the Temple of Jerusalem; but this material realization was imperfect and was destined to be destroyed. The true house of David and the true house of God are constructed together through the death and resurrection of Christ. This occurs thanks to an unexpected synthesis and harmony, as often happens in the Bible where the mystery of Christ is concerned.

In the story of Solomon, we see a clear distinction between

two aspects of the oracle: God had promised David a house, that is, a son who would succeed him; Solomon is this son. The other aspect of the oracle is that this son would have to construct a house for God. So Solomon constructed a Temple at Jerusalem. However, Solomon and the Temple remained two quite distinct realities. On the contrary, the risen Christ is the kingly house given by God to David and, at the same time, the house of God, constructed for God, that is, by the Son of David. Christ is both things together. Christ is the kingly house whose victory over death was achieved by a descendant of David; the Messiah king who reigns forever; therefore, in Jesus, God has given to David a house that will reign forever. On the other hand, Jesus, raised from the dead, is the new house of God since in his Paschal Mystery, Christ has substituted the Temple made by man's hands for a Temple not made by man's hands – and constructed in three days. This was foretold in the Gospels (*Mk* 14:58; *Jn* 2:19). I recalled this when speaking of the Tent not made by human hands.

The body of Jesus, which is restored to life by the Holy Spirit, has become the true house of God, that is, the authentic Temple, the true spiritual house in which all men are invited to enter so as to be in intimate relationship with God. In fact, all are invited to take part and to become living stones. In the expression "spiritual house", the adjective "spiritual" needs to be understood in the powerful sense of the work of the Holy Spirit. Thanks to "the sanctifying action of the Spirit" of which St Peter spoke in the beginning of his Letter (*1 Pt* 1:2), believers play a part in this spiritual house. The Apostle expresses a vigorous dynamism. The movement of Christians who come near to Christ continues in the movement of the building of the spiritual house that is being constructed and this house needs a holy priesthood that consists in the offering of spiritual sacrifices. In this way, we are invited to enter into the powerful dynamism of the offering of Christ. By means of incorporation into Christ, we Christians are consecrated priests and invited to offer. Altogether, we form a "priestly organism", as St Peter says, who – as I said at the beginning of this reflection – uses the word of the Septuagint. In the Book of Exodus, God had made Israel a very beautiful promise: "If you hear my voice and keep my Covenant, you will be to me a kingdom of priests and a holy nation" (19:5). In the Hebrew text we find the word *kohen,* which means priest, in its plural form in the expression "a kingdom of priests" *mamleket kohanim.* The translators of the Septuagint had rendered this with a singular collective, «ιεράτευμα» – "priestly organism" and this is used by St Peter, because it expresses the ecclesial aspect of Christian participation in Christ's priesthood. Christians are not priests singularly, that is, each person on his own and unrelated to the rest. Unfortunately, this is a Protestant perspective that was propagated by Luther. All Christians play a role in the priestly organism. After a profound study of the Letter of St Peter, a Lutheran exegete, J. H. Elliott, very honestly concluded that the individualistic Lutheran interpretation is unsustainable. Participation in Christ's priesthood is ecclesial, not individual. It is personal for each one, but it is not individual.

St Peter specifies that the baptismal priesthood is exercised by the offering of spiritual sacrifices. He does not mean mental sacrifices, that is, a mere intention to offer oneself to God; he means the offering of one's own concrete existence under an impulse given by the Holy Spirit and in docility to him. Christian worship consists in becoming: "Be holy yourselves in all your conduct" says St Peter (*1 Pt* 1:15). "Love one another earnestly from the heart" (*1 Pt* 1:22; 4:8). This goes for every state of life: "Each has received a gift, employ it for one another, as good stewards of God's varied grace" (*1 Pt* 4:10).

In chapter 2 verse 5, the phrase of St Peter expresses the doctrine of the baptismal priesthood of all believers which is the principal aspect of the priesthood of the Church. The contrary could be easily presumed, namely, that the more important aspect would be the ministerial or ordained priesthood. However, this is not correct; several magisterial documents have reaffirmed this recently. The ministerial priesthood is at the service of the baptismal priesthood. This is its aim. The ministerial priesthood is the means, and it is certainly an indispensable means, that is of fundamental significance. Without the ministerial priesthood, the baptismal priesthood cannot to be exercised. However, without the baptismal priesthood of all believers, the ministerial priesthood would lose its meaning. Furthermore, it is necessary to observe that the baptismal priesthood is the priesthood of all the baptized from the smallest to the greatest. We also, who have received the sacrament of Orders, are called to exercise the baptismal priesthood throughout our life, that is, to offer ourselves in union with the offering of Christ. This is an exercise of the baptismal priesthood. In the exercise of our ministerial priesthood, we are called to exercise the baptismal priesthood at the same time. The exercise of both must go together. When we exercise our ministry, we must also offer ourselves in union with the offering of Christ. For us, the baptismal priesthood is more important than the ministerial priesthood. The ministerial priesthood is the gift of Christ to the Church. It is an extraordinary gift. It is not something that belongs to us personally; nor does it increase our personal value. Like all believers, the most important thing for us is the way in which we offer ourselves. It also needs to be said that, for us, this exercise of the baptismal priesthood takes a specific form, namely, one of pastoral charity. The baptismal priesthood is always an exercise of charity but, for us, pastoral charity is the specific, daily and concrete determination of this exercise. Our lives must unite baptismal and ministerial priesthood. However, it is possible to separate them. Unfortunately, this happens. It is possible for an ordained priest to celebrate the Holy Mass without uniting himself personally to the sacrifice of Christ. In that case, he will have exercised his ministerial priesthood; the Mass will have been valid and will have given to the faithful the possibility of exercising their baptismal priesthood by offering themselves in union with the offering of Christ, but the priest himself will not have exercised it, and this is abnormal; even worse, it is scandalous.

St Peter concludes that thanks to the resurrection of Jesus, our life is transformed. He says, "Declare the wonderful deeds of him who called you out of darkness into his marvellous light. Once you were no people but now you are God's people; once you had not received mercy but now you have received mercy" (cf. *1 Pt* 2:9-10). In this way, St Peter invites us all to live united to the mystery of Christ, in grateful love and in the generous offering of our lives. Let us ask him for the grace to correspond well to this invitation of the Apostle.

17
The priestly heart of Christ and the ordained priesthood

Eminences, Excellencies, Monsignors, in conclusion to these spiritual exercises, I now propose to you some modest reflections on the relationships which exist between the ministerial priesthood and the priestly heart of Christ. These relationships are very close because the New Covenant, for the service of which the priesthood is ordered, has the heart of Christ for its centre and source. In the Letter to the Hebrews, in making the comparison between the priesthood of the Old Covenant and that of the New Covenant, it is noted that the priesthood of the Old was external, devoid of a relationship with the heart. In the Old Testament, the heart of the king is often spoken of: Solomon, for example, asks God to give him "a docile heart", that is, "*an understanding mind*" (*1 K* 3:9) and the Book of Proverbs says that "the King's heart is a stream of water in the hand of the Lord" (*Pr* 21:1). The heart of the priest, on the contrary, is never mentioned; the old worship had no relationship to the heart. The Law defined the worship; it was performed by means of conventional, external rites; the immolations of animals were offered. The priest had to fulfil the rites and nothing more.

Jesus has substituted this external and conventional worship with a personal and existential worship that starts from his heart. The priesthood of Christ brings about the New Covenant that consists in the gift to believers of a new heart into which a new Spirit is poured, namely: the Holy Spirit. In establishing the New

Covenant, Jesus accepted a sacrificial transformation of his heart, precisely so as to make of it a new heart. In the New Covenant, the problem of the priesthood and of worship is a problem of the heart; in order to come near to God, it is necessary to have a heart that is worthy of God, one that is purified, holy, truly open and docile to the relationship with God and to the love which he gives. The sad realization of the whole Old Testament is that this heart did not exist: the hearts of all had been led astray and there was no one who was truly just. All have been stained by sin and are, therefore, far from the Lord and unworthy of a relationship with him because their heart is not perfect. In an oracle of Jeremiah, God promised a transformation of the heart, saying (paraphrased): "Behold, the New Covenant will be like this: I will write my Laws on their hearts". A Law written on stone could not bring about true union between God and his people. As such, it was presented as being external both to God and to the people. A prophecy of Jeremiah announces, therefore, that the believers will have a docile heart that will be ready to accomplish the will of God with love; it will be a heart that is disposed to enter into profound and authentic relationship with God. In expressing the same thing but in a more radical way, Ezekiel, in God's name, promised a new heart and a new spirit since it was not enough to write the Law of God on an old heart; the heart needed to be radically changed. Therefore, God said: "A new heart I will give you and a new Spirit I will put within you; and I will take out of your flesh the heart of stone and give you a heart of flesh" (*Ez* 36:26,27).

In order to receive the Spirit of God, it is indispensable to have a new heart. According to the Bible, the Spirit is received in the heart. Therefore, the problem was one of having a human heart that was fully opened to the Spirit of God and disposed to a true covenant with Him, without putting any obstacles in the way. We can see in the Letter to the Hebrews that Jesus has accepted the transformation of his heart so as to bring about this promise of God, that is, to produce a new heart. In a certain sense, the heart of Jesus was a perfect heart even from the beginning. It was united to the Father and disposed to sacrifice itself for men; it is a human heart that has, nevertheless, accepted a transformation in order to fully realize God's design and to be able to communicate to us a new heart. It seems to me that the mystery of redemption is precisely this. The Son of God has taken human nature that bore the mark of sin – as St Paul says, "...the likeness of sinful flesh" (*Rm* 8:3). Otherwise, human nature would have had no need of an interior transformation. He has assumed it precisely so as to effect this transformation of the heart and to obtain for man a new heart. This heart would be docile to God and open to his love, which is also for others.

This transformation has been effected in the passion of Jesus. We all know that Jesus' passion was a moment of great suffering, of great sorrow and of interior struggle. This was especially true of his agony. In it, we see that Jesus truly had a human heart that was exposed to suffering and anxiety; in this anxiety and anguish, he assumed an attitude of complete docility to the Father: "Not mine, but your will be done" and this for the salvation of the brethren. Jesus assumed all the pain of the passion as an occasion of an extraordinary docility of his own heart to the will of the Father. The Letter to the Hebrews says that: "He learned obedience through what he suffered" (*Hb* 5:8). He willed to learn, not for his own sake, but for us, so as to form in himself a docile heart on which the Law of God could be written. Furthermore, this heart would be completely new. It wants nothing else but to obey the Father, to do his will and to put oneself at his disposal for the salvation of the brethren. We must seriously consider what Jesus has accomplished in the redemption: he has truly accepted that his heart would suffer profoundly so as to be transformed and then to be at the disposal of all believers as a new heart that communicates to us a complete openness to God and to the brethren. Here is the priesthood of Christ: Christ is priest and as such is the Mediator of the New Covenant that consists in the transformation of the heart. Jesus has become the perfect priest thanks to his passion, by means of which his human heart was transformed. This heart would become the centre and the source of the New Covenant.

When we speak of the heart of Christ, we are indeed at the centre of the revelation of the New Testament. It not only concerns a theoretical revelation. It also concerns a divine accomplishment that is effected in the human heart of Jesus. We do not really allow ourselves to reach this point; we tend to remain superficial and unable to fully appreciate the richness of the redemption that now lies at our disposal in this new heart. The great revelation is precisely the love that is manifested in the Incarnation of the Son of God and in his passion. Without love, the passion would have no value. It would have been just a tragic and scandalous event. All has been transformed from the interior, that is, from the heart. That which was most externally opposed to love has become the occasion of the greatest love, thanks to the generosity of the heart of Jesus. It is not possible to imagine more contrary circumstances for a development of love: the injustice, the cruelty, the betrayal, all the things which are opposed to love – these have become the occasion of the greatest love in the context of an extraordinary victory. The secret is in the heart of Jesus, that is, in his love.

When we speak of the heart, we speak of love. However, this is a love experienced by a man; it is not a divine love that precedes the Incarnation but a love experienced by the Son of God in his human nature, involving human suffering, human feelings and affections and even human decisions. It concerns a heart that is so generous that it accepts the most contrary circumstances in which to make love superabundant.

St Paul also demonstrates that this is the centre when he speaks of *agape*, that is, of the love of charity (*1 Co* 13). For the Corinthians, there were other things that seemed more interesting and more important than charity, namely: prophecy, extraordinary charisms, the gift of tongues, the *gnosi* or knowledge. All these things seemed more important to them, more divine. St Paul did not hesitate; he said, "Knowledge has no value apart from love, 'knowledge puffs up but love builds up'" (*1 Co* 8:2); "If I have not love", I have nothing. Moreover, "I am nothing" (*1 Co* 13:2). Paul has put love at the centre, which has its own source in the heart of Christ.

The whole of the New Testament continues in this sense and more precisely, in the sense of the union of the two dimensions of love: love for God and love for the brethren. This is the most specific point of the New Testament. The Old Testament already required the love of God "with all one's heart", but did not unite the love of God with the love of neighbour so closely (cf. *Ex* 32:26-29). There was a joining, but it was not as strong as Christ required it to be. As I have already said, in Christ there are two dimensions of the cross, namely: the vertical dimension that expresses relationship with God; and horizontal dimension, which expresses relationship with us. These form a unity: they are the two dimensions of love, united at the centre of the heart of Jesus which intimately unites these two dimensions in spite of the extreme tension which it undergoes. In this way, his heart has become a priestly heart, the heart of the High Priest, the heart of the Mediator of the New Covenant.

The ordained priesthood is the sacrament of Christ's priesthood. It is the sacrament of Christ's priestly mediation. Through the bishops and the priests, Christ makes his priesthood present as the mediation of the New Covenant. Through it, he makes his heart available to all. Therefore, the ordained priesthood has an intimate and even profound relationship to the heart of Christ. It is possible to call it "the sacrament of the priestly heart of Jesus". Christ, the Mediator of the New Covenant, exercises his mediation, which is established in his heart, through "the ministers of the New Covenant" as St Paul says (*2 Co* 3:6). Christ, the good Shepherd, who has loved even to the point of giving his own life for the sheep, takes care of his flock through the shepherds of his Church who are called to "tend the flock of God", as St Peter says in his first Letter (*1 Pt* 5:2) and as St Paul also says in a discourse of the Acts of the Apostles (*Acts* 20:28).

The ordained priesthood, like all the sacraments, is an extraordinary creation of Christ and an expression of his love. Of course, the most important sacrament is the Eucharist, but the Eucharist is not possible without the priesthood. In the Eucharistic celebration, there is not only the body and blood of Christ; there is also the sacramental presence of Christ in the priest. This is a reason for wonder and amazement! We see that Christ has created his sacramental presence, not only in objects and substances, but also in our persons, although they are unworthy. We must be so conscious of this and have such a sense of our responsibility.

As the sacrament of Christ the Priest, the bishop and the priest must be united to the heart of Christ in his two fundamental dispositions, namely: docility toward God and mercy toward men. He must have a filial heart toward God his Father and a fraternal heart toward human persons. Mediation is exercised between two parties and requires that the mediator have good relationships with both. A priestly mediation involves bringing the people into relationship with God. Therefore, for the mediator, there must be, on the one hand, a good relationship with God and, on the other hand, a good relationship with his human brethren. These relationships are fostered when the mediator is concerned for the mediation between God and men and, particularly, when this concern is heartfelt.

Jesus spoke explicitly about a "gentle and lowly" (*Mt* 11:29) heart. A lowly heart is one that is docile to God and filial even to the obedience of the cross. A gentle heart is one that is both fraternal and merciful. When Jesus defines his own heart as gentle and lowly, he touches upon these two aspects of priestly mediation. He reveals his heart to be priestly. A priestly heart is one that unites a humble and docile relationship with God to a gentle and merciful relationship with the brethren. When the Letter to the Hebrews defines the priest, it similarly expresses the content of these two essential qualities, namely: lowliness of heart before God in profound docility (*Hb* 5:45) and gentleness of heart toward the brethren in profound mercy (*Hb* 5:2). Christ's filial heart is manifested in his agony in Gethsemane; there we see Jesus become docile to the Father with immense love; he has made himself lowly. The fraternal heart of Christ was manifested above all in the institution of the Eucharist when Jesus gave himself as the food of fraternal communion. However, in the agony, it is not possible to separate these two aspects. In that moment, Jesus also manifests himself as our brother because he takes all our anxiety on himself, that is, our desperate situation, becoming "like his brethren in every respect" (*Hb* 2:17). In the Eucharistic institution, Jesus also shows himself to be a Son who gives thanks to the Father and receives from him an outpouring of love that is necessary for changing the situation. So we see sonship and fraternity intimately united and these are the two fundamental virtues of the priestly heart of Christ. Therefore, the heart of the priest is defined by the union of these two dispositions: filial docility and fraternal mercy.

Jesus wanted to unite his Apostles to these two fundamental relationships of his heart. With the relationship with the Father, we see Jesus' insistence in saying that he has come not to do his own will, but to do the will of the Father (*Jn* 5:30; 6:38). We see, above all, that he wants to unite the Apostles to his disposition of complete docility. We see it in the agony, when he asks the Apostles to stay awake with him and says: "Stay awake and pray" (*Mt* 26:41). Previously, he had often insisted on the necessity of being docile to the Father; when he is put to the test, he begs the Apostles to share this temptation and this disposition and gives them an unsettling lesson concerning the full docility of filial love, because his cry "Your will be done" (*Mt* 26:42) is not an expression of resignation, but a cry of filial love.

On the other hand, he wanted to unite the Apostles to his heart in his mercy toward sinners. We often see this in the Gospels, in particular, in the calling of Matthew. Matthew was considered to be a sinner because he was a publican. Jesus showed him his surprising mercy, by saying: "Follow me" (*Mt* 9:9). This is an extraordinary honour; he is not only considered by Jesus to be someone to save, but also as a possible co-operator. Immediately after, it is seen that this call of Matthew was the occasion to show that the Apostles must be merciful to sinners and that the disciples of Jesus must be merciful: Matthew organized a banquet with other publicans. This awakens the criticism of the pharisees who said to the Apostles: "Why does your Master eat with publicans and sinners?" Jesus responds decisively: "I have not come to call the just but sinners". Jesus recalls the prophecy of Hosea: "Go and learn what this means, 'I desire mercy, and not sacrifice'" (*Mt* 9:11-13). The Apostles are in this way associated with the movement of mercy in Christ's heart, even from the moment of their calling. No longer will the external ritual worship of sanctification by means of separations be sought after; this is the old system. Now the new worship will be effected in a movement of mercy toward the brethren in full docility to the love of the Father. The sacrifice of Christ was in no way a sacrifice according to the old manner. It was an act of extreme mercy, that is, a capital punishment transformed by the heart into an offering of mercy.

It is also possible to analyze the priesthood in another way. The priesthood of Christ brings together the three dimensions that correspond to its three functions. These are the three *munera*: that of prophet, priest and king. This becomes part of the perspective of the Letter to the Hebrews concerning Christ's priesthood because:

1. Christ communicates the Word of God better than the prophets; after all, he *is* the Word. God has spoken

to us in the Son and now the Word of God comes to us through Christ. This is a fundamental aspect of his priesthood.

2. As priest, Christ sanctifies us by communicating the divine life to us.

3. As king, Christ governs the Church and assures it communion in unity.

These three *munera* belong to the priesthood of Christ the High Priest and are communicated to the ordained priests who must communicate the Word of God as the fundamental aspect, who must communicate the divine life through the Sacraments and who must assure unity in governing the people of God. We can see in the Gospels that in accomplishing these three priestly responsibilities, Jesus wants to associate the Apostles with his heart. We see in the Gospel of Mark that for Jesus, his teaching, that is, his communication of God's Word, is an act of priestly mercy. The evangelist writes: "As he went ashore he saw a great crowd, and he had compassion on them, because they were like sheep without a shepherd; and he began to teach them many things" (*Mk* 6:34). Jesus teaches because he is moved by the situation of the people. This affective aspect of mercy is the source of his teaching activity with which he associates the Apostles (*Mt* 28:19, 20). He must be present in the teaching of the priests and of the bishops. It is not possible to communicate the Word of God if it is not in union with the heart of Christ, that is, with the compassion of Jesus and with his priestly mercy.

The second of the *munera* is to communicate the divine life. This was illustrated in the Gospels in the episodes of the multiplication of loaves. Late in the day, the Apostles asked Jesus to dismiss the people so that going into the villages nearby, they might be able to buy something to eat: "They need not go away; you give them something to eat" (*Mt* 14:16). The task of communicating life is given to the Apostles. Jesus also proves his compassion for the people who risk fainting along the way.

He takes the few loaves available, gives thanks, breaks them and gives them to his disciples that they might distribute them (*Mk* 8:1-6). In this way, Jesus associates his disciples with his attitude of generous love that wants to communicate life. These scenes clearly prefigure the Eucharistic gift. The Gospels make this relationship clear. At the Last Supper, Jesus has placed his own body and blood into the hands of the Apostles and, later, his bishops and priests, so that they might distribute the divine life to all the faithful. This comes from his compassion, from his heart. It is clear that the Eucharist is the most extraordinary gift of the heart of Jesus. Jesus makes his own heart available to the priests who have the mission "to distribute" this heart, just as he has broken the bread and distributed it. Jesus gives his own heart, so that the priests may be able to give it to others and to communicate this extraordinary gift. Fundamentally, the Christian life consists in receiving the heart of Christ.

The third aspect is to assure communion in unity. This aspect is expressed in the Gospel of Matthew which begins with a description of the ministry of Jesus himself saying: "Jesus went about all the cities and villages, teaching in their synagogues and preaching the Gospel of the kingdom, and healing every disease and every infirmity" (*Mt* 9:35). Afterwards, Jesus notes the human dispersion (*diaspora*) and "feels compassion". Again, "When he saw the crowds, he had compassion for them, because they were harassed and helpless, like sheep without a shepherd" (*Mt* 9:36). His heart is moved. He then wants to associate the disciples with his great work of gathering together the human race. "Then he said to his disciples 'The harvest is plentiful but the labourers are few; pray therefore the Lord of the harvest to send out labourers into his harvest'" (*Mt* 9:37-38).

The mission of the twelve is recounted immediately after (*Mt* 10:1-5) and is found in this light. It is understood to be a result of the compassion of the heart of Jesus for the crowds and of his desire to associate chosen men with this charitable work of gathering them together.

This is precisely one of the essential tasks of the priesthood: to structure and pattern unity and to make this unity possible. However, this is not possible without an explicit reference to the heart of Jesus; that is, to the love of Christ expressed from his human heart.

To gather men and women together in the Church and to govern cannot be a work of ambition or of domination. It must be a service inspired by the love of Jesus. Jesus himself said this to the Apostles when they quarrelled for first place:

> You know that those who are supposed to rule over the Gentiles lord it over them, and their great men exercise authority over them. But it shall not be so among you; but whoever would be great among you must be your servant, and whoever would be first among you must be the slave of all. For the Son of Man also came not to be served but to serve, and to give his life for a ransom for many (*Mk* 10:42-45; cf. *Lk* 22:25-26).

In all these examples, we see that the ordained priesthood has been constituted by a call to an intimate union with the heart of Jesus. It seems to me that it is more important to speak of "union with the Heart of Jesus" than of "worship of the Sacred Heart". Certainly, the worship of the Sacred Heart has been approved by the Church and is therefore a very positive element, but it seems to me that the desire of the heart of Jesus is, above all, for union with his heart and not so much the worship of his heart. This latter can have an external aspect which is not interiorly satisfying. Union with the heart of Jesus, on the contrary, would appear to be the essential thing for the exercise of the ministerial priesthood. We must ask the Lord to give us this intense union with him in filial love for the Father and in fraternal love for all those entrusted in our ministry.

Appendix
Discourse of His Holiness Pope Benedict XVI at the conclusion of the Spiritual Exercises of the Roman Curia

Redemptoris Mater Chapel, Saturday, 16th February, 2008

Dear Brothers,

At the end of these days of Spiritual Exercises, I would like to give a heartfelt thanks to you, Your Eminence, for your spiritual guidance that has been offered with such theological competence and spiritual depth. From my angle of vision, I have been able to see, on the wall of the Chapel, the image of Jesus kneeling before St Peter in order to wash his feet. Through your meditations, this image has spoken to me. I have recognized that precisely here, in this attitude, in this act of extreme humility, the new priesthood of Jesus is realized. It is realized in his act of solidarity with us, with our weaknesses, our suffering, our temptations, even to the point of death. I have also seen the red vestments of Jesus with new eyes that speak to me of his blood. You, worthy Cardinal, have taught us that the blood of Jesus was, on account of his prayer, "oxygenated" by the Holy Spirit. In this way, it has become the power of resurrection and the source of life for us. But I could not help meditating also on the figure of St Peter with his outstretched finger. It is the moment in which he begs the

Lord to cleanse not only his feet but also his head and his hands. It seems to me that it expresses – beyond that moment – the difficulty that St Peter and all the disciples of the Lord had in understanding the surprising newness of the priesthood of Jesus, which is his self-abasement and solidarity with us. In this way, he gains for us access to the true Sanctuary, that is, the risen body of Jesus.

Throughout the time of his discipleship and, it seems to me, until his own crucifixion, St Peter would always have needed to listen afresh to Jesus so as to enter more profoundly into the mystery of his priesthood, that is, of the priesthood of Christ which was communicated to the Apostles and their successors.

In this sense, the figure of Peter seems to me to be the figure of all of us in these days. You, Eminence, have helped us to hear the voice of the Lord and to learn again what your and our priesthood is. You have helped us to enter into participation in Christ's priesthood and, in this way, to receive also the new heart, that is, the heart of Jesus, as the centre of the mystery of the New Covenant.

Thank you for all this, Your Eminence. Your words and meditations shall accompany us in this time of Lent on our way toward the Pasch of the Lord. In this sense, I wish all of you, dear brothers, a good Lent, one that is spiritually fruitful, so that we can truly arrive at Easter with an ever-deeper participation in the priesthood of our Lord.

BENEDICT XVI

At the conclusion of the spiritual exercises of the Roman Curia
Redemptoris Mater Chapel
Saturday, 16th February, 2008

Lightning Source UK Ltd.
Milton Keynes UK
06 April 2011

170452UK00001B/171/P